The Final Atonement

Chinedu Daniel Obasi

TEACH Services, Inc.
PUBLISHING
www.TEACHServices.com • (800) 367-1844

World rights reserved. This book or any portion thereof may not be copied or reproduced in any form or manner whatever, except as provided by law, without the written permission of the publisher, except by a reviewer who may quote brief passages in a review.

The author assumes full responsibility for the accuracy and interpretation of the Ellen White quotations cited in this book. Unless otherwise indicated, all scripture quotations are taken from the King James Version of the Bible.

The ESV® Bible (The Holy Bible, English Standard Version®). ESV® Text Edition: 2016. Copyright © 2001 by Crossway, a publishing ministry of Good News Publishers. The ESV® text has been reproduced in cooperation with and by permission of Good News Publishers. Unauthorized reproduction of this publication is prohibited. All rights reserved.

Copyright © 2018 Chinedu Daniel Obasi

Copyright © 2018 TEACH Services, Inc.

ISBN-13: 978-1-4796-0914-7 (Paperback)

ISBN-13: 978-1-4796-0915-4 (ePub)

Library of Congress Control Number: 2018942079

Table of Contents

Foreword v

Preface vii

Introduction ix

Chapter 1—Life Through The Blood 11

Chapter 2—The Image Of The Master Plan 18

Chapter 3—The Man At The Altar 34

Chapter 4—Daily Atonement 43

Chapter 5—Yearly Atonement 47

Chapter 6—Believers And Judgment 55

Chapter 7—The Glorious Heavenly Court 67

Chapter 8—Open And Shut Door 85

Chapter 9—The Vision Of The Evening And Morning 99

Chapter 10—The People Of The Covenant 111

Chapter 11—Prophetic Time 123

Chapter 12—October 22, 1844 129

Chapter 13—The Final Atonement 139

Bibliography 149

Foreword

The Final At-one-ment with God is a most profound revelation of God's redeeming grace. This book speaks of a passionate God who is willing to restore you to your rightful place and give you a second chance.

It is argued that Christ lived in the flesh, died on the cross, rose from the dead, ascended to heaven, and sits on the right hand of the throne of God in heaven. These thoughts must remain visible in the faith of every Christian.

Further, that this same Jesus is a High Priest at the right hand of the throne of Majesty must be an eternal element in the faith of every Christian. This will make such a faith true and full. This book dispels the darkness and brings the light shining forth through Christ's heavenly ministry.

I highly recommend this book to all ministers of the gospel, laymen, members of the body of Christ, and every true seeker of God. It is not a book to be read, but studied and applied as you search and meditate on the Bible.

Indeed, Evangelist Chinedu Daniel Obasi has done a good work by creatively and painstakingly putting these truths together. My prayer is that the thoughts shared in this book will be a blessing to the readers.

Pastor Gaius A. Umahi, PhD
Associate Professor, New Testament Studies and Gender Issues,
Babcock University
WAD Biblical Research Committee Member

Preface

Dear brothers and sisters, *The Final Atonement* (or Final "At-One-Ment" with God) is a revelation of Christ's final work of grace—preparing and perfecting the saints of God in the final hours of probationary time for the church and world. Solemn are the scenes connected with this closing work of atonement. Momentous are the interests involved therein. In the following words we read this serious appeal:

> **And I saw another angel fly in the midst of heaven, having the everlasting gospel to preach unto them that dwell on the earth, and to every nation, and kindred, and tongue, and people, Saying with a loud voice, Fear God, and give glory to him; for the hour of his judgment is come: and worship him that made heaven, and earth, and the sea, and the fountains of waters. (Revelation 14:6–7)**

Today, God's final appeal is going out to every nation, kindred, tongue, and people, with all the tenderness, gentleness, and eagerness which only the love of God makes possible. This is the call that comes to you now with this book in your hand. What you are about to read takes you to heaven's Supreme Court and shows you how divine justice is made available to you. What an amazing adventure! May God richly bless you in your journey for truth.

CHINEDU DANIEL OBASI

Introduction

Dear friends, do you know that God's divine purpose for you is to dwell with Him in heaven? He will not be satisfied until we dwell in heaven with Him. Therefore, it is the privilege of every Christian to not only look for, but also hasten the coming of our Lord Jesus Christ, as we are admonished in the following verse: "Looking for and hasting unto the coming of the day of God, wherein the heavens being on fire shall be dissolved, and the elements shall melt with fervent heat" (2 Peter 3:12).

Having seen God's great plan for us, how shall we be ready to welcome Him? What shall we do to inherit eternal life? In this book, you're about to learn God's plan of salvation like you never saw it before. Jesus said, "I am the way, the truth, and the life: no man cometh unto the Father, but by me" (John 14:6).

> *In this book, you're about to learn God's plan of salvation like you never saw it before.*

King David rhetorically asked, "Thy way, O God, is in the sanctuary: who is so great a God as our God" (Ps. 77:13)? With Jesus being the way and God's way being in the sanctuary, this might suggest that the symbols of the sanctuary point to Christ. With that said, let's get ready because this is truly awesome. Jesus says there's only one way into the kingdom, and that is through Him. We are going to explore this throughout the book.

Chapter 1

Life Through The Blood

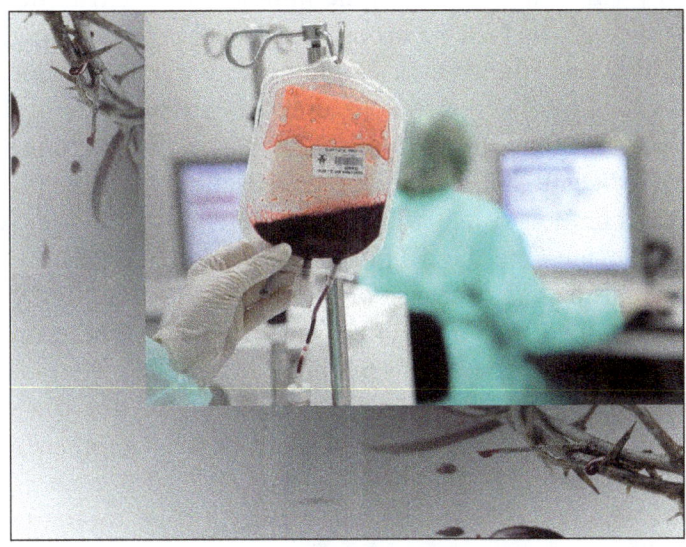

Blood is the red liquid that circulates through the arteries and veins, carrying oxygen to and carbon dioxide from the tissues of the body. Our lives are dependent on blood. Whenever we breathe in full, deep inhalations of pure air, it fills our lungs with oxygen, which purifies our blood and imparts to it a bright color; thus the life-giving current is sent to every part of our body.

As the physical life of the body is sustained by blood, so our spiritual lives are sustained through faith in the precious blood of Jesus. **"For the life of the flesh *is* in the blood: and I have given it to you upon the altar to make atonement for your souls: for it *is* the blood *that* maketh atonement for the soul"** (Lev. 17:11).

This chapter takes us through God's divine purpose in setting up the sanctuary—His plan and wishes concerning humanity's salvation from sin through Jesus Christ, His only begotten Son.

Here we have a great prophecy of a holy place prepared by the hands of God, to which His people were to be brought, so they might have free access to the atoning blood of Christ and thus be made pure for God Himself to dwell as an abode. And that's why the scripture says:

"For thus saith the high and lofty One that inhabiteth eternity, whose name *is* Holy; I dwell in the high and holy *place*, with him also *that is* of a contrite and humble spirit, to revive the spirit of the humble, and to revive the heart of the contrite ones" (Isa. 57:15).

Through Isaiah's inspired record, the Lord reveals how from eternal ages the abode of the Divine Presence was in the high and holy place of the heavenly sanctuary, as well as the humble and contrite hearts of His created beings. It was God's purpose that every created being, from the bright and holy ser aph to man, should be a temple for the indwelling of the Creator. Therefore, the temple, erected as the abode of the Divine Presence, was designed to be an object lesson for Israel and the world.

However, because of sin, humanity ceased to be a temple for God. Darkened and defiled by evil, the heart of humanity no longer reveals the glory of the Divine One. God's purpose and plan is to restore humanity back to its rightful state. Because of the Father's love for and yearning to have communion with us, a way out was provided. Where on earth did God promise to dwell among His people?

"Thus saith the LORD, The heaven *is* my throne, and the earth *is* my footstool: where *is* the house that ye build unto me? And where *is* the place of my rest" (Isa. 66:1)?

"And let them make me a sanctuary; that I may dwell among them" (Exod. 25:8).

"Then said Solomon, The LORD hath said that he would dwell in the thick darkness. But I have built an house of habitation for thee, and a place for thy dwelling for ever" (2 Chron. 6:1–2).

God's plan has a greater purpose than just the building of a temple or a restoration of a building to its original condition. His purpose is much greater. His promise reaches far into the hearts of humanity. What has always been God's purpose in relation to His people? **"And I will dwell among the children of Israel, and will be their God"** (Exod. 29:45).

God's eternal purpose is to dwell among us and unite with us by a vital connection. Just as the branch is united with the vine, so we are to be united with our Maker. He wants to return humanity to the perfection of character possessed by Adam and Eve before their fall into sin.

To Israel, among whom He desired to make His dwelling place, He revealed His glorious ideal of character. All who love the worship of God and prize the blessing of His sacred presence will manifest the same spirit of sacrifice in preparing a house where God may meet with them.

The Covenant of Grace

It is interesting to note that after the fall, the covenant of grace was made with Adam and Eve in Eden. They were given a divine promise about the coming seed of the woman which shall bruise the serpent's head. **"And I will put enmity between thee and the woman, and between thy seed and her seed; it shall bruise thy head, and thou shalt bruise his heel"** (Gen. 3:15).

God's Word has revealed to us that there's going to be a spiritual battle between four principal figures:

1. **The serpent**
2. **The woman**
3. **The seed of the woman**
4. **The seeds of the serpent**

The woman represents the church and the seed represents Christ (see 2 Cor. 11:2; Eph. 5:31, 32; Gal. 3:16). The serpent is the devil and the seeds of the serpent are his followers (see Rev. 12:9). The woman, in the primary sense, represents God's faithful children in all ages, while in the secondary sense, she represents the old covenant and the human phase of the everlasting covenant. However, the Seed (Christ) represents the new covenant and the divine phase of the everlasting covenant.

The covenant of grace is not a new truth, for it existed in the mind of God from eternity past. This is why it is called the everlasting covenant. Long before God made a covenant with Israel, He first made a covenant with Adam, Noah, and Abraham.

The covenant made with Abraham 430 years before the law was spoken on Sinai was a covenant confirmed by God in Christ—the very same gospel which is preached to us. **"And the scripture, foreseeing that God would justify the heathen through faith, preached before the gospel unto Abraham, *saying*, In thee shall all nations be blessed. So then they which be of faith are blessed with faithful Abraham"** (Gal. 3:8, 9).

To all men this covenant offered pardon, and the assisting grace of God for future obedience through faith in Christ. It also promised them eternal life on condition of fidelity to God's law. Thus the patriarchs received the hope of salvation. (White, *The Faith I Live By*, p. 77)

Why was the covenant made with Israel called the first covenant when it was by no means the first covenant that God made with humanity? It is because this covenant made with Israel contained all the object lessons and was ratified by the blood of an animal sacrifice. It was a system designed as a schoolmaster to teach us through symbol the import of Christ's redeeming sacrifice.

Dear friends, God's purpose and plan of grace, which existed from all eternity, is called the everlasting covenant, and through the sacrificial services of the Hebrew sanctuary, God designed to reveal the details of His everlasting covenant and plan of redemption.

Make Me a Sanctuary

It would seem, from the expressions the Lord made to Moses concerning the sanctuary, that not only did He show him a mere pattern of the things He wanted him to build, but rather a real sanctuary in heaven. Speaking of this sanctuary, Paul wrote, **"Who serve unto the example and shadow of heavenly things, as Moses was admonished of God when he was about to make the tabernacle: for, See, saith he, *that* thou make all things according to the pattern shewed to thee in the mount"** (Heb. 8:5).

From this text we learn that the earthly sanctuary was built after a real one. The objects in the sanctuary and its services on earth are used as an example or illustration of the things that really are in heaven. The earthly is a mere shadow of the heavenly. There could be no shadow if there was no object itself to cast the shadow.

The term "sanctuary," as used in the Bible, refers primarily to the tabernacle built by Moses and secondarily to a pattern of the heavenly temple, the "true tabernacle" pitched by God in heaven, to which the earthly sanctuary points. It also refers to our bodily temple, or the temple of the human soul. Let's briefly look at the temple of the human soul.

The Temple of the Human Soul

"Know ye not that ye are the temple of God, and [that] the Spirit of God dwelleth in you" (1 Cor. 3:16)? Yes, indeed, our body is the temple of the Most High God. It is the desire of God to make the human soul His dwelling place…His temple…His sanctuary.

That was why, in the beginning, God created male and female in His own likeness. He endowed them with noble qualities. Their minds were well-balanced, and all the powers of their being were harmonious.

It was sin that marred and well-nigh obliterated the image of God in humanity. Sin perverted God's gifts. It was to restore this original design that the plan of salvation was devised, and a life of probation was granted to humanity. To bring people back to the perfection in which they were first created is the great object of life—the object that underlies every other. What plan was devised in the heavenly courts for the restoration of the human soul? **"For we know that if our earthly house of *this* tabernacle were dissolved, we have a building of God, an house not made with hands, eternal in the heavens. For in this we groan, earnestly desiring to be clothed upon with our house which is from heaven"** (2 Cor. 5:1–2).

If there is a human temple, a dwelling place of God within the soul, there should be a heavenly pattern too. The bodily human temple has a pattern of heavenly origin not made by the power of man, but the power of God—after God's own ideal, which was the pattern for all. Hence the Savior, when speaking to the Jews after He cast out the money-changers, replied to the Pharisee who asked for a sign in the following manner: **"Jesus answered and said unto them, 'Destroy this temple, and in three days I will raise it up.' Then said the Jews, 'Forty and six years was this temple in building, and wilt thou rear it up in three days?' But he spake of the temple of his body"** (John 2:19–21).

Here Jesus referred to His body as the temple of God. Thus, we have the lesson that God wanted to teach the Israelites and, through them, all people, concerning the sanctuary. It is on this basis that the following inspired words were written: **"What? know ye not that your body is the temple of the Holy Ghost [which is] in you, which ye have of God, and ye are not your own"** (1 Cor. 6:19)?

We are told that our body is the temple of God, just as was Jesus'. This is the practical lesson the Jewish sanctuary was designed to teach when God's presence in the earthly tabernacle was seen in the form of the holy Shekinah, sanctifying all the ritual services. God aimed to show how He desired to dwell in the temple of our human souls in order to sanctify our lives.

> *To bring people back to the perfection in which they were first created is the great object of life—the object that underlies every other.*

However, there must be a heavenly-human temple which should be a pattern or example for all human temples. Therefore, Jesus Christ, the Lord of heaven, the second Adam, was prepared by God to be our pattern, being the real Temple of God's indwelling presence. He is the One after which every temple must be patterned.

Jesus is the Ideal; He is the real Temple; He is the practical lesson of the sanctuary, the dwelling place of God. **"To whom God would make known what *is* the riches of the glory of this mystery among the Gentiles; which is Christ in you, the hope of glory"** (Col. 1:27).

If Christ is in us, we will have Christ's character in us. If Christ is in our flesh, we will reveal His glory—the Skekinah glory, the Most Holy presence. God's plan is to make each one of us a sanctuary so He can dwell in us, and as God filled Christ with the Holy Spirit without measure, so God designed that all shall be filled with His Holy Spirit. Please note that the Bible clearly presents four sanctuaries:

1. **The earthly sanctuary**
2. **The heavenly sanctuary**
3. **The human body (the temple of the Holy Spirit)**
4. **The body of our Lord Jesus Christ (The dwelling of the fullness of God in bodily form)**

The Purpose of the Sanctuary

The sanctuary is more than just a framework for sacrificial rituals; it teaches us what God is like and other heavenly realities. God does not like long-distance relationships. He desires a personal relationship with each of His creatures. In order for Christ to dwell in us, we must experience the following:

> **Then will I sprinkle clean water upon you, and ye shall be clean: from all your filthiness, and from all your idols, will I cleanse you. A new heart also will I give you, and a new spirit will I put within you: and I will take away the stony heart out of your flesh, and I will give you an heart of flesh. And I will put my spirit within you, and cause you to walk in my statutes, and ye shall keep my judgments, and do *them*. And ye shall dwell in the land that I gave to your fathers; and ye shall be My people, and I will be your God.** (Ezek. 36:25–28)

The Sanctuary of the New Covenant

As we begin this study, it is interesting to note that when Paul was freely discussing the subject of the sanctuary in the book of Hebrews, he clearly stated that the sanctuary and its typical system pertained to the first covenant. **"Then verily the first *covenant* had also ordinances of divine service, and a worldly sanctuary"** (Heb. 9:1). He called the sanctuary of the first covenant, with its ordinances and priestly services, a figure of the heavenly, into which Christ Himself entered when He ascended to heaven. **"*It was* therefore necessary that the patterns of things in the heavens should be purified with these; but the heavenly things themselves with better sacrifices than these. For Christ is not entered into the holy places made with hands, *which are* the figures of the true; but into heaven itself, now to appear in the presence of God for us"** (Heb. 9:23–24).

Thus, when Jesus ascended to the right hand of the Father in the heavens, He became a minister of the sanctuary and the true tabernacle. David recognized that there is a heavenly sanctuary, which is why he wrote, **"For he hath looked down from the height of his sanctuary; from heaven did the LORD behold the earth"** (Ps. 102:19).

From the above reference, we see that the sanctuary of the new covenant is not on earth, but in heaven. Therefore, the new covenant tabernacle was made and pitched by the Lord in contradistinction to that of the first covenant, which was made and pitched by humans in obedience to the command of God.

Christ's intercession—associated with which are His pierced and broken body, spotless life, wounded hands, pierced side, marred feet, and pleading blood—is a work of ministration that was purchased at such an infinite cost. The correct understanding of this ministration in the heavenly sanctuary under the new covenant is the foundation of our faith.

Chapter 2

The Image of the Master Plan

After the Lord gave Moses the command to build the sanctuary, what plan was shown him? **"According to all that I shew thee, *after* the pattern of the tabernacle, and the pattern of all the instruments thereof, even so shall ye make *it*"** (Exod. 25:9). He gave him specific directions for the building of all its parts—its furniture within and decorations without.

After what was the Mosaic tabernacle patterned? **"Now of the things which we have spoken *this is* the sum: We have such an high priest, who is set on the right hand of the throne of the Majesty in the heavens; A minister of the sanctuary, and of the true tabernacle, which the Lord pitched, and not man"** (Heb. 8:1–2). The earthly sanctuary was pattern after the heavenly reality. Every part had a special function, and in every manner it must be made according to the pattern.

No Heavenly Sanctuary

As some are trying to prove that there is no real sanctuary in heaven, the argument is brought forth that Moses simply made it according to how the Lord showed it, not according to what he saw in heaven. In other words, when Moses was on the mount, he was viewing a panoramic view, or picture, of what the Lord wanted, not necessarily what was really there. However, let's take a closer look at this subject. Speaking of this, Paul wrote the previous verses.

Notice how toward the end of verse 2, he specifically said that the Lord pitched the tabernacle, not man. We know that humans did pitch sanctuaries, didn't they? Of course—during Moses' era, as well as Solomon's era and the post-exile era. Does this mean that Paul is either confused or being dishonest?

Of course not! He is striking a contrast between what involved human intervention and what involved only divine involvement. Moreover, if there is no heavenly sanctuary, there cannot be a heavenly High Priest. Let us continue in verse 2. The first part says, **"A minister of the sanctuary, and of true tabernacle…"**; who is the person who ministers in the sanctuary? Who is that High Priest? It is Jesus Christ (see Heb. 7:22–28).

If Jesus is ministering in the sanctuary, and the earthly temple does not exist today since it was destroyed in AD 70, it follows that He is ministering in a sanctuary that is in heaven. Furthermore, we read this in verse 5: **"Who serve unto the example and shadow of heavenly things, as Moses was admonished of God when he was about to make the tabernacle: for, See, saith he, *that* thou make all things according to the pattern shewed to thee in the mount."**

Notice the first clause in the verse. If God just showed Moses a picture, what heavenly things is Paul referencing?

Compare this with what is said in Hebrews 9:1: **"Then verily the first *covenant* had also ordinances of divine service, and a worldly sanctuary."** If there is no heavenly sanctuary, why would Paul speak of a worldly sanctuary? We further read in verse 11: **"But Christ being come an high priest of good things to come, by a greater and more perfect tabernacle, not made with hands, that is to say, not of this building;"** if there was only one sanctuary made, the earthly one, why does he now speak about one being greater and more perfect? These words make it necessary for there to be an inferior, less perfect sanctuary. Thus, we have two sanctuaries—a greater one and a lesser one. Of course, the greater one would be the one in heaven, where all things are great.

"**For Christ is not entered into the holy places made with hands, *which are* the figures of the true; but into heaven itself, now to appear in the presence of God for us**" (v. 24). This verse says Christ did not enter a holy place made with hands. The phrase "made with hands" is translated from the Greek word *cheiropoietos*, which means "manufactured of human construction." This means Christ did not enter the earthly sanctuary, which was made by humans, but rather the heavenly sanctuary, which was made by God. Notice that the earthly sanctuary was a "figure" (or "representative") of the true the heavenly sanctuary.

A Metaphorical Application

Inasmuch as we cannot deny the fact that there is a real, antitypical sanctuary in heaven, which Moses was shown as a pattern, and a real ministry of Jesus, which was typified by the earthly ministry in Israel's various temples, we also cannot overlook the metaphorical applications of some of the sanctuary elements and services. Besides the pattern, what (or who) else metaphorically reflects the sanctuary?

As we already read, David said that God's way is in the sanctuary and Jesus said He is the Way! Putting those concepts together would suggest that Jesus is the One who metaphorically reflects and is interwoven throughout all the symbols of the sanctuary. Let's see if that is true.

The Sanctuary Gate

Beginning with the entrance gate, where is Christ in this sanctuary component? There is only one gate into the sanctuary court, and that gate was the only way through which people entered. Who does it typifies? Jesus said, **"I am the door: by me if any man enters in, he shall be saved, and shall go in and out, and find pasture"** (John 10:9). Jesus is the door to our salvation. He is the only way to God. We are told, **"Neither is there salvation in any other: for there is none other name under heaven given among men, whereby we must be saved"** (Acts 4:12).

Therefore, Jesus is the only way into God's Kingdom, and that's what the only entrance into the sanctuary court typifies. Did you notice that the entrance to the sanctuary enclosure was at the eastern end? Since the entrance was at the eastern end, that means their backs would be towards the sun. The Most Holy Place was towards the west. This illustrates that it is God we are to worship, not the creation, such as how pagan cultures worship the sun.

Dear friends, always remember the sanctuary is an expansive parable designed to teach us about the plan of salvation—the gospel message. As wax takes the impression of the seal, so the temple is to take the impression of the Spirit of God and retain the image of Christ.

There were three parts to the earthly sanctuary built by Moses—the outer court, the Holy Place, and the Most Holy Place. What services were conducted within each of these parts?

Outer Court

The sacred tent was enclosed in an open space called the courtyard. Surrounding the court was a wall (with an entrance, of course) made of fine-hanging linen, supported by pillars. The court enclosed the sanctuary, and the entire territory was pitched in the center of the encampment of the Israelites. "And thou shalt make the court of the tabernacle: for the south side southward *there shall be* hangings for the court *of* fine twined linen of an hundred cubits long for one side: And the twenty pillars thereof and their twenty sockets *shall be of* brass; the hooks of the pillars and their fillets *shall be of* silver" (Exod. 27:9–10).

Pillars

What do the pillars represent? The Bible says, "Wisdom hath builded her house, she hath hewn out her seven pillars" (Prov. 9:1). Who in the Holy Scriptures is the embodiment of wisdom? "But unto them which are called, both Jews and Greeks, Christ the power of God, and the wisdom of God" (1 Cor. 1:24). Jesus is the wisdom of God, a treasure which is as lasting as eternity. To all who believe in Jesus as the One able to save unto the uttermost all that come unto God by Him, the gospel is power and wisdom.

Of whoever gains victory over every besetment of the enemy, lays hold of this power that is out of and beyond oneself, and thus maintains a constant, living connection with Christ, the Bible says, "will I make a pillar in the temple of my God, and he shall go no more out: and I will write upon him the name of my God, and the name of the city of my God, *which is* new Jerusalem, which cometh down out of heaven from my God: and *I will write upon him* my new name" (Rev. 3:12).

Here the redeemed or overcomers are represented as pillars in God's temple. It does not imply that they were literal, physical blocks or stones holding up the temple, but rather the subject of God's grace, emblem of His great love and sacrifice, and token of His triumph.

In order to gain victory over every sin, we must lay hold of a power that is out of and beyond ourselves. We must maintain a constant, living connection with Christ, who has the power to give victory to every soul that will maintain an attitude of faith and humility.

As those who hope to receive the overcomers' reward, we must press forward in the Christian warfare. Though at every advance we meet with opposition, we are to overcome through the blood of the Lamb and the word of our testimony, and thus become qualified to be pillars in the temple of our God.

The Brazen Altar of Sacrifice

The first object you see as you enter the outer court of the sanctuary is the altar of sacrifice. The altar consisted of a brazen grate which kept the sacrifice lifted above the ground.

> *When you come to Jesus and confess your sins to Him, He takes your sins and punishment upon Himself and gives you a new life.*

While we are in the "outer court," what "living sacrifices" are we required to offer on the altar? **"Your lamb shall be without blemish, a male lamb of the first year"** (Exod. 12:5). We are to place upon the altar a spotless offering. Every offering brought as a sacrifice to God must be carefully examined. If any defect was discovered in the animal presented, it was refused. The penitent must confess their sins upon its head, symbolically transferring them to the animal before it is sacrificed on the altar in our stead.

In the same manner, Jesus Christ, the spotless Son of God, was offered to bear the sins of the world. Speaking of Jesus, John the Baptist said, **"Behold the Lamb of God, which taketh away the sin of the world"** (John 1:29).

The one great sacrifice made for us is found in the life, mission, and death of Jesus Christ. The value of Christ's offering consists of the fact that He is the Son of God, as well as the Son of man; also, that He is sinless—a perfect sacrifice with no need of an offering for Himself (see Heb. 7:27); and that it is voluntary on his part (see John 10:17). When you come to Jesus and confess your sins to Him, He takes your sins and punishment upon Himself and gives you a new life.

The Four Horns

The altar of sacrifice has four horns. What do horns represent? Horns are the chief weapons and ornaments of the animals that possess them. Hence, the word "horn" is often used to signify strength, honor, and victory, as well as power. "And hath raised up an horn of salvation for us…" (Luke 1:69); "he had horns…there was the hiding of His power" (Hab. 3:4).

Even the sacrifice was tied to the horns. In ancient Israel, horns were grasped by desperate people as a means of refuge. If you were chased by enemies for the wrong reason, and you were innocent, you could run to the refuge, but if you could not find the refuge nearby, if you could run into the courtyard and hold the horns of the altar of burnt offering, and you were safe. No one could come in and kill you unless you were judged and proven guilty, in which case you could not be protected (Joab was an example). "But if a man come presumptuously upon his neighbour, to slay him with guile; thou shalt take him from mine altar that he may die" (Exod. 21:14). When Joab was in trouble, he "fled unto the tabernacle of the LORD, and caught hold on the horns of the altar" (1 Kings 2:28).

This was like taking hold of Jehovah's strength for protection. However, Joab was guilty, and even though he was grasping the horns, the soldiers came in and killed him right in the courtyard. He was just pretending that he was innocent.

Yes, if you come to Jesus Christ at the foot of the cross and say, "I repent and confess my sins. You know my heart Lord" and hold onto the strength and power of His blood, you are saved. It's a refuge, and Satan cannot touch you.

Yet, if you are pretending—cherishing sins in your heart—God cannot protect you from the pursuit of Satan. That is the lesson—touching the horns means forgiveness and holiness for the sincere, penitent people.

The horn represents the power of salvation. What is the power of God unto salvation? "For I am not ashamed of the gospel of Christ: for it is the power of God unto salvation to everyone that believeth; to the Jew first, and also to the Greek" (Rom. 1:16).

The four horns also point to the universal power in the gospel (consider that there are four cardinal directions: north, south, east, and west). "And Jesus came and spake unto them, saying, All power is given unto me in heaven and in earth" (Matt. 28:18). After the cross, He was given all power. The power of His sacrifice is providing salvation to the four corners of the earth. The Bible says that He is "not willing that any should perish, but that all should come to repentance" (2 Peter 3:9).

Speaking further of this, the Apostle John wrote, "And I beheld, and, lo, in the midst of the throne and of the four beasts, and in the midst of the elders, stood a Lamb as it had been slain, having seven horns and seven eyes, which are the seven Spirits of God sent forth into all the earth" (Rev. 5:6). Seven stands for completeness and perfection. What are the seven Spirits? **"And the spirit of the LORD shall rest upon him, the spirit of wisdom and understanding, the spirit of counsel and might, the spirit of knowledge and of the fear of the LORD"** (Isa. 11:2).

The Prophet Isaiah listed six spirits:
1. **Wisdom**
2. **Understanding**
3. **Counsel**
4. **Might**
5. **Knowledge**
6. **The Fear of the Lord**

What is the seventh spirit? **"The Spirit of the Lord GOD *is* upon me; because the LORD hath anointed me to preach good tidings unto the meek; he hath sent me to bind up the brokenhearted, to proclaim liberty to the captives, and the opening of the prison to *them that are* bound; To proclaim the acceptable year of the LORD"** (Isa. 61:1, 2).

The Laver and Its Use

The next item you see in the outer court is the laver. **"Thou shalt also make a laver *of* brass, and his foot *also of* brass, to wash *withal*: and thou shalt put it between the tabernacle of the congregation and the altar, and thou shalt put water therein"** (Exod. 30:18).

The laver was located between the altar and the door of the Holy Place. The purpose of the laver was for the priests to wash their hands and feet before they entered the Holy Place to minister, or before they offered any burnt offering unto the Lord. Thus, you can see that the only place where cleansing was done was at the laver. The laver must always be supplied with water, so that the priest will have enough on hand whenever it was needed.

The laver and all the washings and sprinklings enjoined in the ceremonial law were lessons in parables, teaching the necessity of the work of regeneration in the inward heart for the purification of the soul that's dead in trespasses and sins, as well as the sanctifying power of the Holy Spirit. The psalmist declares, **"I will wash mine hands in innocency: so will I compass thine altar, O LORD"** (Ps. 26:6). Also, **"Purge me with hyssop, and I shall be clean: wash me, and I shall be whiter than snow"** (Ps. 51:7).

David appreciated its meaning and saw at least one lesson that it taught. In this symbol, we find a representation of being washed from sin and receiving a new life in Christ. Water in the Bible is also a symbol of the Holy Spirit. **"In the last day, that great *day* of the feast, Jesus stood** and cried, saying, If any man thirst, let him come unto me, and drink. He that believeth on me, as the scripture hath said, out of his belly shall flow rivers of living water. (But this spake he of the Spirit, which they that believe on him should receive: for the Holy Ghost was not yet *given*; because that Jesus was not yet glorified)" (John 7:37–39).

With that said, the question is how does this relate to the washing ritual of the sanctuary service? The Bible says, "Not by works of righteousness which we have done, but according to his mercy he saved us, by the washing of regeneration, and renewing of the Holy Ghost" (Titus 3:5). "Jesus answered, Verily, verily, I say unto thee, Except a man be born of water and *of* the Spirit, he cannot enter into the kingdom of God" (John 3:5). "Therefore we are buried with him by baptism into death: that like as Christ was raised up from the dead by the glory of the Father, even so we also should walk in newness of life" (Rom. 6:4).

The washing is connected to regeneration—a spiritual rebirth; that was why on the cross, both blood and water flowed from the side of Christ. In the courtyard of the sanctuary, we find the water and the blood. Both pardon and cleansing are offered to all who will believe. A new life, with new desires and tendencies, will be the result. The Bible says, "If we confess our sins, he is faithful and just to forgive us *our* sins, and to cleanse us from all unrighteousness" (1 John 1:9).

The laver points to Jesus as the One who cleanses us and makes us acceptable before the very presence of our great God. Friends, it is a marvelous revelation to know that the entire sanctuary service was symbolic of Christ.

The Holy Place

Next, as you enter into the sanctuary, there are two compartments containing various pieces of furniture. Let's see how each one represents Jesus. The first apartment of the sanctuary building is called the Holy Place. There are three articles of furniture, the first of which being the table of a show bread standing on the north side, with twelve loaves of bread that are arranged in two heaps. This bread was to be eaten only by the priests. It was called the bread of His presence because it was continually before the face of Jehovah.

The Table of Showbread

The Bible says, "And thou shalt set upon the table shewbread before me alway" (Exod. 25:30). On this table, the priests were to place twelve cakes of fresh bread each Sabbath, arranged in two heaps. The loaves that were removed, being accounted as holy, were to be eaten only by the priests. It was continually before the face of Jehovah. How many beautiful lessons are taught here by the Holy Spirit?

The bread here represents Christ, who is the Bread of Life with which He feeds the people. This we find recorded in many instances. The reason it is called the bread of the presence is because it is He who is always in the presence of God and delegated by God to feed humanity with His own life and power. The showbread was designed to teach us to feed upon Jesus as the Everlasting Word. **"For the bread of God is he which cometh down from heaven, and giveth life unto the world.... And Jesus said unto them, I am the bread of life: he that cometh to me shall never hunger** (John 6:33, 35). **"I am the living bread which came down from heaven: if any man eat of this bread, he shall live for ever: and the bread that I will give is my flesh, which I will give for the life of the world"** (v. 51).

Christ came down from heaven—from the very bosom and presence of the Father—to feed people with the Bread of Life. The twelve loaves might be associated with the twelve tribes of Israel (and perhaps the twelve apostles also), whom He separated for Himself as a distinct and peculiar people, guardians of His truth, keepers of His law, and depository of His sacred oracles.

The Golden Candlestick

Another beautiful article of furniture was the seven-branched golden candlestick. The Bible says: **"And thou shalt make the seven lamps thereof: and they shall light the lamps thereof, that they may give light over against it"** (Exod. 25:37). It was on the south side. There were no windows in the tabernacle, so the purpose of the candlestick was to give light. It must be lighted every day, constantly supplied with oil, and have its wicks trimmed each morning. Great care always needed to be taken so that it would never become useless.

The Apostle John saw the seven golden candlesticks in heaven, and the Savior said they were illustrative of the seven churches. **"The mystery of the seven stars which thou sawest in my right hand, and the seven golden candlesticks. The seven stars are the angels of the seven churches: and the seven candlesticks which thou sawest are the seven churches"** (Rev. 1:20).

What is the mission of the church? When Christ was in the world, He said He was the light of the world. By extension, He told the church that she was the light of the world. **"Let your light so shine before men, that they may see your good works, and glorify your Father which is in heaven"** (Matt. 5:16).

The light must come from the oil that furnished the candlestick. The candlestick is the bearer, the oil is the feeder, and the snuffers the trimmer. This was God's plan. Likewise, Jesus Christ is the Light bearer to the world—to every individual soul; the Holy Spirit is the oil; His blessed and precious Word does the trimming. This thought is forcibly brought out in the parable of the ten virgins.

The Golden Altar of Incense

Still another interesting article of furniture in the sanctuary was the altar of incense. **"And thou shalt make an altar to burn incense upon"** (Exod. 30:1). Just in front of the inner veil, which separated the Holy Place from the Most Holy Place, stood the golden alter of incense. Upon this alter the priest burned incense every morning and evening at the hours of prayer.

If you have noticed, there are only two altars (burnt sacrifices and incense). These altars that both burn something are squared, not rectangular. The latter is the tallest piece of furniture in the Holy Place. As part of the sanctification process, what brings us closer to God heavenward? The Bible says, **"And thou shalt put it before the vail that *is* by the ark of the testimony, before the mercy seat that *is* over the testimony, where I will meet with thee"** (v. 6).

As in that typical service, the priest looked by faith to the mercy seat, which he could not see; so in like manner, the people of God are now to direct their prayers to Christ, their Great High Priest who, unseen by human vision, is pleading on their behalf in the sanctuary above. In the vision that John wrote, he mentioned a very beautiful golden altar that he saw in heaven, and described it this way: **"And another angel came and stood at the altar, having a golden censer; and there was given unto him much incense, that he should offer *it* with the prayers of all saints upon the golden altar which was before the throne. And the smoke of the incense, *which came* with the prayers of the saints, ascended up before God out of the angel's hand"** (Rev. 8:3, 4).

In heaven, right by the throne of God, stands a golden altar, the true altar of which the earthly was a type. We are also informed that on this altar was offered incense, even as on the altar in the earthly temple. What is the composition of the incense, and what does it symbolize?

Incense

Exodus 30:34 lists the different ingredients, each of which may carry some import. For example, the Hebrew word for "frankincense" is *lebonah* (known for whiteness), which comes from *libbah*, which means "heart." In the LXX, the Greek means "oozing substance," usually understood as a product of myrrh ("bitterness"). This perfume has the savor of bitterness. What is the spiritual meaning of incense? Here is what the psalmist says: **"Let my prayer be set forth before thee *as* incense"** (Ps. 141:2; in verse 1, David is crying unto the Lord).

In other words, (frank)incense is a prayer that is offered from a sincere heart—the confession of sinners, made with remorse, regret, and the savor of bitterness of a broken and contrite spirit.

This incense, however, was added to the prayers of the saints of God as they were offered up by the angel. We are told that we do not know how to pray. Hence, our own prayers, in raw form, cannot reach the throne of God. **"Likewise the Spirit also helpeth our infirmities: for we know not what we should pray for as we ought: but the Spirit itself maketh intercession for us with groanings which cannot be uttered"** (Rom. 8:26).

The incense, ascending with the prayers of Israel, with the moist drops of the blood of Christ, represents His merits, intercession, and perfect righteousness, which, through faith, is imputed to His people and alone can make the worship of sinful beings acceptable to God. What a beautiful truth this altar was designed to teach!

The Curtain of Separation

Just in front of this ark, the Lord commanded Moses to hang a very beautiful curtain made of blue, purple, scarlet, and fine-twined lined, and designed with embroidered figures of cherubim. This was to form a partition between the two apartments, since no one was permitted to enter into the Most Holy Place at any time (for this was punishable by death), except the high priest, and he only on the Day of Atonement. Having already seen that all the articles of the earthly sanctuary were but shadows of the heavenly, the veil or door which separated the two apartments must be a shadow or type of some heavenly reality.

That there were two apartments in the heavenly sanctuary is apparent from the types themselves. One very precious, practical lesson from the veil is referenced by Paul: **"Having therefore, brethren, boldness to enter into the holiest by the blood of Jesus, By a new and living way, which he** hath consecrated for us, through the veil, that is to say, his flesh" (Heb. 10:19–20).

Yes, Jesus is the door. He is the veil, and through Him we can come before the mercy seat into the presence of God.

The Most Holy Place and the Ark

The Most Holy Place contained one article of furniture: the ark of the covenant. This was a wooden chest overlaid with gold. In it were two tables of stone upon which was written the law of God, the Ten Commandments, as well as a pot of manna and Aaron's rod that budded.

What lesson was to be taught by the ark, with its contents? First of all, Webster's Dictionary defines the word "ark" as a vessel of safety or refuge. It is well-known how arks had been used at different periods of world history prior to this time. There are three arks in the Bible, all of which were designed as vessels of safety. First is Noah's ark (see Gen. 6), built at a period when the Lord was to bring a flood upon the world. Noah was commanded to enter into the ark as a vessel of refuge for him and his family.

Second, we have the ark that Jochebed made for baby Moses (see Exod. 2:3). When Moses was born, it was expected that he would be killed according to the command of pharaoh, so his mother secured him in an ark and hid him in a pool. Last but not least is the ark of the covenant.

The Mercy Seat and the Cherubim

"And thou shalt make a mercy seat *of* pure gold: two cubits and a half *shall be* the length thereof, and a cubit and a half the breadth thereof" (Exod. 25:17). This was to be of pure gold, and its position was above the ark, functioning as a lid. It was to be a solid piece of fine gold, and on each end stood the figure of an angel or covering cherub.

> And thou shalt make two cherubims *of* gold; *of* beaten work shalt thou make them, in the two ends of the mercy seat. And make one cherub on the one end, and the other cherub on the other end: *even* of the mercy seat shall ye make the cherubims on the two ends thereof. And the cherubims shall stretch forth *their* wings on high, covering the mercy seat with their wings, and their faces *shall look* one to another; toward the mercy seat shall the faces of the cherubims be. (Exod. 25:20)

These angels stood with uplifted wings, as if in worship. Above the mercy seat, between the cherubim, appeared the supernatural bright light called the Shekinah, the visible manifestation of Jehovah's presence among His people. The Bible says, **"And there I will meet with thee, and I will commune with thee from above the mercy seat, from between the two cherubims which *are* upon the ark of the testimony, of all *things* which I will give thee in commandment unto the children of Israel"** (v. 22).

The Ten Commandments

When God instructed Moses to build the earthly sanctuary, He commanded him to "Make it after the pattern." However, there was one exception. When it came to writing the law of the Almighty Father, God essentially said, "Moses, I'll do this." Notice His words: **"And he gave unto Moses, when he had made an end of communing with him upon mount Sinai, two tables of testimony, tables of stone, written with the finger of God"** (Exod. 31:18).

Everything found within the earthly sanctuary was made by men, except the Ten Commandments. These were written in stone by the immortal finger of God Almighty. After placing the law in the ark, what happened next? **"And he took and put the testimony into the ark, and set the staves on the ark, and put the mercy seat above upon the ark"** (Exod. 40:20).

The cover of the ark was called the mercy seat because mercy and pardon were granted to the repentant sinner whenever the blood of an offering was sprinkled before and upon it, thus honoring and satisfying the claims of the holy law underneath, which had been transgressed.

Pot of Manna

"Then said the LORD unto Moses, Behold, I will rain bread from heaven for you; and the people shall go out and gather a certain rate every day, that I may prove them, whether they will walk in my law, or no" (Exod. 16:4). From this text, we are told that God rained down bread from heaven upon the ancient Israelites during their journey from Egypt to Canaan. The psalmist confirmed this phenomenon: **"And had rained down manna upon them to eat, and had given them of the corn of heaven. Man did eat angels' food: he sent them meat to the full"** (78:24–25).

In the ark, beneath where the angels' wings were spread, was a golden pot of manna, of a yellowish cast. Jesus said to the Jews, **"Your fathers did eat manna in the wilderness, and are dead...I am the living bread which came down from heaven: if any man eats of this bread, he shall live forever: and the bread that I will give is my flesh, which I will give for** the life of the world" (John 6:49, 51). Here we are told that Jesus is that very bread that came down from heaven, and that whoever eats Him shall live forever. Jesus further explained: **"It is the Spirit that quickeneth; the flesh profiteth nothing: the words that I speak unto you,** *they* **are spirit, and** *they* **are life"** (v. 63).

The Word of Christ is the bread of life that is furnished for every soul that lives. To refuse to eat this bread is death. Whoever neglects to partake of the Word of God shall not see life. From where did manna come? It was not food that they could cultivate. It was not food that they could sow or reap. The manna came down from heaven. That means that our spiritual food—the Word of God, the Bible—is not something that we can make or create. It fell down from heaven through the merits of Jesus Christ. What we have to do is simply go out, gather and cook what was needed, and eat for our spiritual nourishment. Where did manna fall?

Manna fell only on the territory of Israelites. It did not fall in Moab, Egypt, or among the Philistines. If you want to find manna, be among spiritual people. They did not travel many miles to gather it. They didn't have to drive one or two hours to get manna every morning, No! It fell around their tents, in the morning, as they woke up.

Do you have to drive one hour every morning to get manna? Do you have to travel thousands of miles to get the bread of life from heaven? No! When you get up, it's there around you. If you want to have it, it's there. While we are fed spiritually with the Word of God today, God's promise to overcomers is this: **"He who has an ear, let him hear what the Spirit says to the churches. To him who overcomes I will give some of the hidden manna to eat. And I will give him a white stone, and on the stone a new name written which no one knows except him who receives it"** (Rev. 2:17, NKJV).

Aaron's Rod

Aaron's rod **"brought forth buds, and bloomed blossoms, and yielded almonds"** (Num. 17:8). Aaron's rod represents Christ's high priestly ministry. **"And there shall come forth a rod out of the stem of Jesse, and a Branch shall grow out of his roots"** (Isa. 11:1).

"The LORD shall send the rod of thy strength out of Zion: rule thou in the midst of thine enemies…The LORD hath sworn, and will not repent, Thou *art* **a priest for ever after the order of Melchizedek"** (Ps. 110:2, 4).

Christ was the chosen Leader—the true Messiah. Just as Aaron's dead rod brought forth life, Christ rose again from the tomb. The almond tree is the first tree that buds after the winter. It fitly represents Christ, **"the firstfruits of them that slept"** (1 Cor. 15:20).

Aaron's rod was even used to swallow up the Pharaoh's magicians' serpents. Christ swallowed up death and gained power over Satan. The rod was used to perform miracles. It also represents God's chosen people. The Bible says, **"Remember thy congregation,** *which* **thou hast purchased of old; the rod of thine inheritance,** *which* **thou hast redeemed; this mount Zion, wherein thou hast dwelt"** (Ps. 74:2). **"The portion of Jacob** *is* **not like them; for he** *is* **the former of all things: and** *Israel is* **the rod of his inheritance: the LORD of hosts** *is* **his name"** (Jer. 51:19).

What do you need to experience? We are all dried, dead rods with sinful, carnal minds and deteriorated bodies. However, if we are laid in the sanctuary with the experience thereof, God is going to perform a miracle for you and me and make these dry, dead rods bloom, bud, and even yield crop.

Once again, we see the Lord's desire for us to be in harmony with His law and partake of the manna of His Word every day. Thus, we shall eat of the hidden manna from heaven because God has chosen us to be a part of the royal priesthood. Amen!

What is the spiritual lesson in all this? What can we learn from the pot of manna and the Aaron's rod? Also, what can we learn from the mercy seat? The Scripture says, **"Sacrifice and offering thou didst not desire; mine ears hast thou opened: burnt offering and sin offering hast thou not required. Then said I, Lo, I come: in the volume of the book** *it is* **written of me"** (Ps. 40:6, 7).

Who is the focus of this prophecy? **"Wherefore when he cometh into the world, he saith, Sacrifice and offering thou wouldest not, but a body hast thou prepared me: In burnt offerings and** *sacrifices* **for sin thou hast had no pleasure. Then said I, Lo, I come (in the volume of the book it is written of me,) to do thy will, O God"** (Heb. 10:5–7).

Thus, we see the fulfillment of this prediction is none other than Jesus Christ. God prepared Him a body. Why? **"I delight to do thy will, O my God: yea, thy law** *is* **within my heart"** (Ps. 40:8).

Jesus was prepared a body in which the law of God was deposited. Where in Him was the law deposited? The law of God was deposited in His heart and reflected through His whole life. Thus, the fleshly tables of His divine-human soul were inscribed by the finger of God's own hand with the divine and eternal precepts of His unalterable law.

Then it must be apparent that the ark, the vessel of safety, was also a symbol of the life of Christ in which was placed the law of Jehovah.

Therefore, Christ's heart was the safe and secure place for the law of God to abide. This also points to the work Jesus wants to accomplish in us. The Bible says, **"This *is* the covenant that I will make with them after those days, saith the Lord, I will put my laws into their hearts, and in their minds will I write them; And their sins and iniquities will I remember no more. Now where remission of these *is*, *there is* no more offering for sin. Having therefore, brethren, boldness to enter into the holiest by the blood of Jesus"** (Heb. 10:16–19).

The ark of the covenant is evidence of God fulfilling His ultimate promises—writing His law in our hearts, blotting out sin, and giving us complete victory, even over the grave. The fact that Christ's own heart and our hearts are also represented by the ark of God, where He puts His law, does not nullify the existence of a heavenly ark.

The Censer

"And he shall take a censer full of burning coals of fire from off the altar before the LORD, and his hands full of sweet incense beaten small, and bring *it* within the vail: And he shall put the incense upon the fire before the LORD, that the cloud of the incense may cover the mercy seat that *is* upon the testimony, that he die not" (Lev. 16:12–13). In the temple service, the Lord gave special directions that the priests were to use in their censers only the sacred fire of God's own kindling, which was kept burning day and night. We also noted that each priest has its own censer. The Bible confirms this: **"And there stood before them seventy men of the ancients of the house of Israel, and in the midst of them stood Jaazaniah the son of Shaphan, with every man his censer in his hand; and a thick cloud of incense went up"** (Ezek. 8:11). **"And take every man his censer, and put incense in them, and bring ye before the LORD every man his censer, two hundred and fifty censers; thou also, and Aaron, each *of you* his censer"** (Num. 16:17).

It is interesting to note that in the Hebrew sanctuary, the censers used in the daily services were of brass, while those used on the Day of Atonement were of gold. The purpose of the censer was to burn incense before the mercy seat on the Day of Atonement. All incense needed to be moist with the drops of the blood of the sin offering when burned during the morning and evening services.

CHAPTER 3

The Man At The Altar

In this chapter, we shall discover that Christ is our High Priest who, previously as the Lamb of God, shed His precious blood on Calvary. This study takes us back to the patriarchal days when the head of every Jewish family was the household priest who ministered for the family before the Lord. The father of the family was supposed to intercede on his family's behalf.

Speaking about Abraham, the Bible says, **"For I know him, that he will command his children and his household after him, and they shall keep the way of the Lord, to do justice and judgment"** (Gen. 18:19).

> The life of Abraham, the friend of God, was signalized by a strict regard for the word of the Lord. He cultivated home religion. The fear of God pervaded his household. He was the priest of his home. He looked upon his family as a sacred trust. (White, *Conflict and Courage*, p. 49)

In the days of Israelites, after they became a nation, the types of the gospel of salvation through the Messiah and the priesthood were confined to a special tribe. The Bible says,

"And the LORD spake unto Moses, saying, And I, behold, I have taken the Levites from among the children of Israel instead of all the firstborn that openeth the matrix among the children of Israel: therefore the Levites shall be mine" (Num. 3:11–12).

The Levites, though divinely set apart to assist the priests, never entered the sanctuary itself, except when the camp was moved from place to place, and even then, only after all the furniture had been covered. At other times, their service was confined to the outer court. Although the tribe chosen was that of Levi, the gift of priesthood was placed upon Aaron and his posterity. **"And thou shalt appoint Aaron and his sons, and they shall wait on their priest's office"** (v. 10).

This priesthood was to be confined only to the family of Aaron, not to be transmitted to any other portion of this tribe. **"And these *are* the names of the sons of Aaron; Nadab the firstborn, and Abihu, Eleazar, and Ithamar. These *are* the names of the sons of Aaron, the priests which were anointed, whom he consecrated to minister in the priest's office"** (vs. 2, 3). The priesthood was divided into two parts: the high priest and the regular priest.

Regular Priest

As you know, the ordinary Israelite only had access to the outer court when he brought his sacrifice for sin. The work of the regular priests was to minister before the Lord, conducting their service in the court and Holy Place and acting as mediators between God and the people.

They were to bring the blood, which was shed by the person through slitting the offering's throat for the forgiveness of sins, and sprinkle it in the Holy Place, just before the veil.

And the elders of the congregation shall lay their hands upon the head of the bullock before the LORD: and the bullock shall be killed before the LORD. And the priest that is anointed shall bring of the bullock's blood to the tabernacle of the congregation: And the priest shall dip his finger *in some* of the blood, and sprinkle *it* seven times before the LORD, *even* before the veil.… And he shall do with the bullock as he did with the bullock for a sin offering, so shall he do with this: and the priest shall make atonement for them, and it shall be forgiven them. (Lev. 4:15–17, 20)

The priest that was anointed to this work carried out his job through the sprinkled blood that was shed, and by bearing the sins in the flesh, he was to make known God's method of atonement. The regular priest never entered the Most Holy Place, because that was not his duty to do so.

What Clear Command Was Given to the Priest?

> **Do not drink wine nor strong drink, thou, nor thy sons with thee, when ye go into the tabernacle of the congregation, lest ye die:** *it shall be* **a statute for ever throughout your generations: And that ye may put difference between holy and unholy, and between unclean and clean; And that ye may teach the children of Israel all the statutes which the LORD hath spoken unto them by the hand of Moses.** (Lev. 10:9–11)

> These words of warning and command are pointed and decided. Let those in positions of public trust take heed, lest thru wine and strong drink they forget the law, and pervert judgment. Rulers and judges should ever be in a condition to fulfill the instruction of the Lord… (White, *The Signs of the Times*, November 20, 1907, par. 11)

It was the use of fermented wine that caused Nadab and Abihu to confuse the sacred and the common, and death was their penalty. Here we have the plainest directions of God and His reasons for prohibiting the use of wine—that their power of discrimination and discernment might be clear and in no way confused; that their judgment might be correct, and they are ever able to discern between the clean and unclean.

How Often Was the Priest to Offer Sacrifices?

> **"The one lamb thou shalt offer in the morning; and the other lamb thou shalt offer at even"** (Exod. 29:39).

> As the priests morning and evening entered the holy place at the time of incense, the daily sacrifice was ready to be offered upon the altar in the court without. This was a time of intense interest to the worshipers who assembled at the tabernacle. Before entering into the presence of God through the ministration of the priest, they were to engage in earnest searching of heart and confession of sin. They united in silent prayer, with their faces toward the holy place. Thus their petitions ascended with the cloud of incense, while faith laid hold upon the merits of the promised Saviour prefigured by the atoning sacrifice.

The hours appointed for the morning and the evening sacrifice were regarded as sacred, and they came to be observed as the set time for worship throughout the Jewish nation. And when in later times the Jews were scattered as captives in distant lands, they still at the appointed hour turned their faces toward Jerusalem and offered up their petitions to the God of Israel. In this custom Christians have an example for morning and evening prayer. While God condemns a mere round of ceremonies, without the spirit of worship, He looks with great pleasure upon those who love Him, bowing morning and evening to seek pardon for sins committed and to present their requests for needed blessings. (White, *Patriarchs and Prophets*, pp. 353–4)

High Priest

During the year, the high priest had duties to perform, not only in the court, but also in the Holy Place, and on the Day of Atonement, his duties led him into the Most Holy Place. Into this apartment he went alone to perform the special services.

"**And *he that is* the high priest among his brethren, upon whose head the anointing oil was poured, and that is consecrated to put on the garments, shall not uncover his head, nor rend his clothes**" (Lev. 21:10).

The oldest son was to succeed his father in the high priesthood when the latter died. If, however, the oldest son died, the next in age was to be the successor.

The High Priest's Miter and Garment

The miter of the high priest consisted of a white linen turban, having attached to it with a lace of blue a gold plate bearing the inscription, "Holiness to Jehovah." Everything connected with the apparel and deportment of the priests was to impress the beholder with a sense of the holiness of God, sacredness of His worship, and purity required of those who came into His presence.

The priests were to have two sets of holy garments made from special material worked in a particular manner. The regular priest has a linen garment, while the high priest owns a robe of beauty and glory. The robe of the common priest was of white linen and woven in one piece. It extended nearly to the feet and was confined about the waist by a white linen girdle embroidered in blue, purple, and red.

A linen turban, or miter, completed his outer costume. Everything worn by the priest was to be whole and without blemish. Those beautiful, official garments represented the character of the Great Antitype, Jesus Christ. Nothing but perfection, in dress, attitude, word, and spirit, can be acceptable to God. He is holy, and His glory and perfection must be represented by the earthly service. Nothing but perfection could properly represent the sacredness of the heavenly service. Finite man might rend his own heart by showing a contrite and humble spirit. This, God would discern.

However, no tear must be made in the priestly robes, for this would mar the representation of heavenly things. The high priest who dared to appear in holy office and engage in the service of the sanctuary with a torn robe was looked upon as having severed himself from God. By rending his garment, he cut himself off from being of a representative character. He was no longer accepted by God as an officiating priest. This course of action, as exhibited by Caiaphas, showed human passion and imperfection.

Likewise, the experience of Christians must be constant as they go steadily forward,

having as his motto: *"this* one thing *I do"* (Phil. 3:13). Faith in Christ, not emotions, must hold us true to duty and loyal to God's everlasting truth. Emotions are unstable, up and down, here and there. Guided by them, we shall be **"like a wave of the sea driven with the wind and tossed"** (James 1:6).

Moses, at the burning bush, was directed to put off his sandals, for the ground whereon he stood was holy. Similarly, the priests were not to enter the sanctuary with shoes upon their feet. Particles of dust cleaving to them would desecrate the Holy Place.

They were to leave their shoes in the court before entering the sanctuary, as well as wash both their hands and feet before ministering in the tabernacle or at the altar of burnt offering. Thereby was constantly taught the lesson that all defilement must be put away from those who would approach the presence of God.

The wearing of these holy garments by the priests **"when they come in unto the tabernacle of the congregation [the Holy Place], or when they come near unto the altar to minister"** (Exod. 28:43) was a very definite requirement of God, and any failure on the part of a priest to obey meant death. Why so severe a penalty? Because in this case, it would be impossible for the priest to bear the iniquity of the children of Israel, which, as Christ's representative, was his role. **"And the LORD said unto Aaron, Thou and thy sons and thy father's house with thee shall bear the** iniquity of the sanctuary: and thou and thy sons with thee shall bear the iniquity of your priesthood" (Num. 18:1).

Consecration of the Priestly Garments

The breastplate, ephod, embroidered coat, miter, and girdle were to be worn by the high priest alone. All these garments were to be specially anointed and consecrated, even as the priest himself was. The garments of the high priest were of costly material and beautiful workmanship, befitting his exalted station. In addition to the linen dress of the common priest, he wore a robe of blue, also woven in one piece. Around the skirt, it was ornamented with golden bells and pomegranates of blue, purple, and scarlet.

It is interesting to note that the bells were made of pure gold, representing great value, rather than something like sounding brass, which might be considered a symbol of a lack of love (see 1 Cor. 13:1). The bells also had a functional purpose on the Day of Atonement. Their joyful sound indicated to the people that the high priest had finished his work in safety and that God had accepted the sacrifice for their sins.

Everything connected with the apparel and deportment of the priests was to impress the beholder with a sense of the holiness of God, sacredness of His worship, and purity required of those who came into His presence.

Pomegranates

Consider some of the features of pomegranates. It has purplish-red shell that is completely packed with seeds, each of which containing a sack of blood-red, delicious, sometimes-bitter juice. Each fruit is a veritable basket of precious seed, which has been paralleled with the Word of God (see Luke 8:11). On average, one pomegranate of ordinary size contains approximately 650 seeds, perhaps suggesting that the Word of God is literally packed with precious promises. The color of the juice resembles the blood of Jesus Christ, which cleanses all sin.

The fine-twined linen made of royal colors of blue, purple, and scarlet perhaps has similar significance. Not only is the scarlet indicative of the sacrificial character and work of Christ, but also the sacrifice of His followers, even unto death, which is often necessary in order to carry the truth of God to those in darkness. The white linen represents not only the righteousness of Christ, but the righteousness required of those whom God calls to His work— **"be ye clean, that bears the vessels of the LORD"** (Isa. 52:11). They sow the precious seed beside all waters, bringing things new and old out of God's Word. **"He that goeth forth and weepeth, bearing precious seed shall doubtless come again with rejoicing, bringing his sheaves** *with him"* (Ps. 126:6).

The Ephod

"And he made the ephod *of* **gold, blue, and purple, and scarlet, and fine twined linen. And they did beat the gold into thin plates, and cut** *it into* **wires, to work** *it* **in the blue, and in the purple, and in the scarlet, and in the fine linen,** *with* **cunning work"** (Exod. 39:2, 3).

Outside the main robe was the ephod, a shorter garment of gold, blue, purple, scarlet, and white. It was confined by a girdle of the same colors, beautifully wrought. The ephod was sleeveless, and two onyx stones, bearing the names of the twelve tribes of Israel, were set on its gold-embroidered shoulder pieces.

The word *ephod* is sometimes translated as "apron." It was artistically embroidered and the costliest and most magnificent of his garments, every thread of which representing the perfect character of Christ. This gorgeous material, richly embroidered with real gold thread, connected the high priest personally and officially with the gate of the court, the door of the tabernacle, the veil, and the beautiful inner covering of the sanctuary, all of which were of the same costly material and skillful workmanship as the ephod was. It was in two parts—one for the front and one for the back. These pieces were joined together at the shoulder by their two edges.

The Two Onyx Stones

"And thou shalt take two onyx stones, and grave on them the names of the children of Israel: Six of their names on one stone, and *the other* **six names of the rest on the other stone, according to their birth"** (Exod. 28:9, 10). The front and back of the ephod were clasped together at the shoulders with two onyx stones. The word for "stones" in the Hebrew is *eben* ("to build"). These stones represented God's desire to build His kingdom.

This is only possible because of the ministry of the High Priest, Jesus Christ. Each stone was to be engraved with the names of six of the twelve tribes of Israel (see Exod. 39:6). It is then stated that the high priest was to regard these stones as a memorial unto the children of Israel and bear their names before the Lord upon his two shoulders. What a beautiful, precious illustration for the kingdom of our Lord and Savior Jesus Christ! The Bible says, "For unto us a child is born, unto us a son is given: and the government shall be upon his shoulder" (Isa. 9:6).

The Breastplate

"And thou shalt make the breastplate of judgment with cunning work; after the work of the ephod thou shalt make it; *of* gold, *of* blue, and *of* purple, and *of* scarlet, and *of* fine twined linen, shalt thou make it" (Exod. 28:15). The breastplate was made of the same precious material as the ephod was. It was a perfect square—the length and width were about nine inches. It was attached to the ephod above the girdle. Beautiful gold chains were attached to it above and below, giving it a rich and gilded appearance.

What made it appear most beautiful were the four rows of precious stones that were inserted into it. Each of the four rows contained three stones twelve total (see vs. 15–29). These stones were similar to the ones that constituted the walls of the beautiful city of God—the New Jerusalem (see Rev. 21:19, 20).

On each stone was a name of one of the tribes of Israel. The breastplate was so worn that it covered the heart, so the high priest figuratively bore Israel upon his heart when he went into the sanctuary to minister before the Lord. In addition to this, there were two other stones in the breastplate, which were called the Urim and Thummim. These were the oracles through which the priest inquired of God, and God answered him.

This illustrates to us the work of the Great High Priest, Jesus, the Son of God, who upon His divine human soul bears the names of all His children in the heavenly sanctuary before the Father. How glad we should be to hear that Jesus our High Priest is today presenting our names before His Father, pleading for us His merit through His precious, shed blood!

Ministry of the Priests

A priest was ordained to act as a mediator. The word "mediator" comes from the Greek *mesites*, meaning "one who intervenes between two," "to restore peace and friendship," "to ratify (confirm) a covenant," etc. Also meaning "advocate," "attorney," or "reconciler," the sanctuary teaches us the need of a mediator.

The earthly priests were ordained to offer sacrifices as mediators between God and humanity. They were to carry the blood from the courtyard to the Holy Place; this was part of the mediation and reconciliation roles of the priest. All of the priesthood is pointing us to the role of Christ Jesus to reconcile us back to God.

The Bible says, **"Who will have all men to be saved, and to come unto the knowledge of the truth. For *there is* one God, and one mediator between God and men, the man Christ Jesus"** (1 Tim. 2:4, 5). God intended that these great leaders of His people should be representatives of Christ. Aaron bore the names of Israel upon his breast. He communicated to the people the will of God and entered the Most Holy Place on the Day of Atonement as a mediator.

The office of the priesthood is a type of Christ's priesthood ministry. During His life, Christ never entered the Holy Place or the Most Holy Place, because His work as a priest did not begin until His sacrificial work in the "outer court" of earth was finished. Then He began His ministry in the Holy Place of the heavenly sanctuary. **"Neither by the blood of goats and calves, but by his own blood he entered in once into the holy place, having obtained eternal redemption *for us*.... For Christ is not entered into the holy places made with hands, *which are* the figures of the true; but into heaven itself, now to appear in the presence of God for us"** (Heb. 9:12, 24).

Just as the priests were to be anointed/sanctified, they were representatives of Christ. In the mission of Christ, we are told, **"And for their sakes I sanctify myself, that they also might be sanctified"** (John 17:19); **"Christ also loved the church, and gave himself for it; That He might sanctify and cleanse it"** (Eph. 5:25, 26); **"Wherefore Jesus also, that he might sanctify the people with His own blood, suffered without the gate"** (Heb. 13:12).

Paul alluded to the purpose of being sanctified: **"And the very God of peace sanctify you wholly; and *I pray God* your body be preserved blameless unto the coming of our Lord Jesus Christ"** (1 Thess. 5:23). Furthermore, mediations consist of reconciliation: **"And, having made peace through the blood of His cross, by him to reconcile all things unto himself...And you, that were sometime alienated and enemies in *your* mind by wicked works, yet now hath He reconciled In the body of His flesh through death"** (Col. 1:20–22). Reconciliation was made possible through the blood of Jesus: **"when we were enemies, we were reconciled to God by the death of His Son"** (Rom. 5:10; see also 2 Chron. 29:24).

Chapter 4

Daily Atonement

The central component in the sanctuary service was the blood of the atonement. All the other services would have been useless if there had not been a way provided for the remission of sins through the blood. The Bible says, **"For the life of the flesh *is* in the blood: and I have given it to you upon the altar to make atonement for your souls: for it *is* the blood *that* maketh an atonement for the soul"** (Lev. 17:11).

To many, it has been a mystery why so many sacrificial offerings were required in the old dispensation; why so many bleeding victims were led to the altar. We are told in the Holy Writings that the life of all flesh is in the blood, and because of this, God has given it to us on the altar to make atonement for our souls. In the old dispensation, there are two types of blood atonement: the first is the daily atonement, while the second is the yearly atonement. In each case, blood was taken into the sanctuary.

In the first atonement, the ordinary priest takes the blood into the Holy Place, while in the second atonement the high priest takes the blood into the Most Holy Place. Why must the blood be taken into the sanctuary? Concerning the sin offering, the Bible says, **"and *God* hath given it you to bear the iniquity of the congregation, to make atonement for them before the LORD"** (Lev. 10:17). Please note, God is telling us that the life of the sin offering is in the blood, and the blood is given to make atonement for our souls on the altar; it carries the sins of the people. Does it carry the sins into the sanctuary? If yes, why? If not, why not?

Blood Application

Before answering that, we should address a bigger question: Why blood? Is there no other way to atone for our sins? The answer is absolutely not! We are told in the Holy Scriptures, **"And almost all things are by the law purged with blood; and without shedding of blood is no remission"** (Heb. 9:22). This divine declaration brings us face to face with the solemn fact that there is no other way for anyone to be saved, but by the shedding of blood. Our next question is this: How does blood remit our sins? Let's go to the sanctuary to answer this question.

> **And if any one of the common people sin through ignorance, while he doeth *somewhat against* any of the commandments of the LORD *concerning things* which ought not to be done, and be guilty; Or if his sin, which he hath sinned, come to his knowledge: then he shall bring his offering, a kid of the goats, a female without blemish, for his sin which he hath sinned.** (Lev. 4:27, 28)

Here we find that the sinner must follow the divine plan to get someone's sins remitted. First, a lamb must be brought to the outer court of the sanctuary, and next we read, **"And he shall lay his hand upon the head of the sin offering, and slay it for a sin offering in the place where they kill the burnt offering"** (v. 33). The sinner must place his hands on the head of the animal and confess his sin over its head. In doing this, he transfers his sins to the lamb, which becomes his substitute. He then takes the lamb, places it on the altar, and with his hand, takes a knife and cuts the throat of the innocent victim.

"And the priest shall take of the blood of the sin offering with his finger, and put *it* upon the horns of the altar of burnt offering, and shall pour out all the blood thereof at the bottom of the altar" (v. 34). After the slaughter, the blood is caught in a bowl. The priest takes the blood, puts his finger in the blood, and touches the four horns of the altar of sacrifices. Then the priest moves into the tabernacle for another round of ceremony. We are told:

> And the priest that is anointed shall take of the bullock's blood, and bring it to the tabernacle of the congregation: And the priest shall dip his finger in the blood, and sprinkle of the blood seven times before the LORD, before the vail of the sanctuary. And the priest shall put *some* of the blood upon the horns of the altar of sweet incense before the LORD, which *is* in the tabernacle of the congregation; and shall pour all the blood of the bullock at the bottom of the altar of the burnt offering, which *is at* the door of the tabernacle of the congregation. (Lev. 4:5–7)

Burning of the Fat

"And he shall burn all his fat upon the altar, as the fat of the sacrifice of peace offerings: and the priest shall make atonement for him as concerning his sin, and it shall be forgiven him" (v. 26). After the blood was sprinkled on the two altars, confessions were made for the penitent sinner by the priest. Forgiveness was then obtained, and the fat of the slain animal was burned up on the altar of sacrifice. The fat represents the person's sin, and the burning typifies the destruction of sinful lust and passions; a death to sin in the flesh; a preparatory work for a newness of life.

The Record of Sin in the Temple

As the sin of the offender was transferred, in figure, to the offering, when the blood was administered, the sin was deposited into the sanctuary itself. Is there anything in the sanctuary service dealing with the priest's activity that is connected to a book or record of sin? The Bible says, "The sin of Judah *is* written with a pen of iron, *and* with the point of a diamond: *it is* graven upon the table of their heart, and upon the horns of your altars" (Jer. 17:1).

Why blood? Is there no other way to atone for our sins? The answer is absolutely not!

The book of record is typified by the altar where the blood is sprinkled. As the blood is life, and in that life was guilt, the presence of blood in the sanctuary was evidence that life had been taken, and through that blood, sin had been recorded in the presence of God.

The service of the sacrifice of expiation went forward day by day through the sanctuary, with its offering of blood applied to the altar of incense and the veil between the Holy Place and Most Holy Place, right before the law of God. It is interesting to note that in the old dispensation, there is a continual transfer of sin from the people to their offerings, then to the sanctuary. Thus, the sins of the Israelites accumulated in the sanctuary, day by day, throughout the year.

Chapter 5

Yearly Atonement

Once a year, on the great Day of Atonement, the high priest enters the Most Holy Place with the blood of a designated offering. This work completes the all year-round, daily atonement carried out by the regular priests. On this day, the people were to afflict their souls while the work of atonement was going forward in the Most Holy Place. This annual Jewish ceremony involves three elements:

1. The blotting out of sins
2. The cleansing of the sanctuary
3. Judgment

The Blotting out of Sins

Under the old covenant, when sins were forgiven on a daily basis, were they completely eliminated at that time? **"Blessed *is he whose* transgression** *is* forgiven, *whose* sin *is* covered" (Ps. 32:1). In the daily sacrifice, the sins of the penitent, by the reason of forgiveness, are covered by the blood of the sin offerings, but were not eliminated or blotted out from the record of the sanctuary.

What does it mean to blot out? The Hebrew word for "blot" is *machah*, and it means "to erase or abolish," "stroke out or put out." In the Old Testament dispensation, the word "blot" is used in connection with the following experiences:

"Have mercy upon me, O God, according to thy lovingkindness: according unto the multitude of thy tender mercies *blot out my transgressions*" (Ps. 51:1, emphasis mine).

"Hide thy face from my sins, and blot out all mine iniquities" (v. 9).

"I have blotted out, as a thick cloud, thy transgressions, and, as a cloud, thy sins: return unto me; for I have redeemed thee" (Isa. 44:22).

Dear friends, can you see that the term "blot" (in its various conjugations) was used in connection with wiping out sin, transgression or iniquity? But wait a minute…where were the sins that needed to be blotted out located? The Bible says, "And cover not their iniquity, and let not their sin be blotted out from before thee: for they have provoked *thee* to anger before the builders" (Neh. 4:5).

We are told that the sins that were to be blotted out are before God. The Bible says, "The sin of Judah *is* written with a pen of iron, *and* with the point of a diamond: *it is* graven upon the table of their heart, and upon the horns of your altars" (Jer. 17:1). Please note there are two places where the records of sins are written: our hearts and God's altar.

This confirms that God's people's sins are transferred into the sanctuary through the blood of the sin offering. By what means are our sins blotted out? The Bible says, "And almost all things are by the law purged with blood; and without shedding of blood is no remission" (Heb. 9:22). This is why we must study what takes place within the sanctuary concerning the sins which have been transferred by virtue of Christ's blood and work of substitution. The Bible says:

"Now when these things were thus ordained, the priests went always into the first tabernacle, accomplishing the service *of God*. But into the second *went* the high priest alone once every year, not without blood, which he offered for himself and *for* the errors of the people" (vs. 6, 7).

Who ministered in the first apartment? The regular priests. How often? Every day. Who went into the Most Holy Place? Only the high priest. How often? Only once a year. What did he take with him? He took blood. You see, the path into the sanctuary is a bloodstained path, and inside there is more blood on the horns of the brazen altar, golden altar, and on the mercy seat.

To reiterate, we are told that the sins of God's people are, through blood, brought into the sanctuary and graven upon the horns of God's altar. How does God blot these sins out from the altar and entire sanctuary?

The Cleansing of the Sanctuary

And he shall make atonement for the holy *place*, because of the uncleanness of the children of Israel, and because of their transgressions in all their sins: and so shall he do for the tabernacle of the congregation that remaineth among them in the midst of their uncleanness....And he shall go out unto the altar that *is* before the LORD, and make an atonement for it; and shall take of the blood of the bullock, and of the blood of the goat, and put *it* upon the horns of the altar round about. And he shall sprinkle of the blood upon it with his finger seven times, and cleanse it, and hallow it from the uncleanness of the children of Israel. (Lev. 16:16–19)

The reason for this was that during the year, the animals which had been slain for the sins of the people had their blood brought into the Holy Place, by which act the records of sins were kept. Of course, this was merely typical and figurative. Nevertheless, these pieces of furniture were affected by the blood which was sprinkled upon them during the year.

Since the blood of the slain, innocent animal carried the sins of the penitent believer, and was emblematic of the life thereof, these vessels shared in the work of liberating the people. Therefore, on the Day of Atonement, when the work of blotting out sin from the nation was completed, the sanctuary was also cleansed from sin and its effects. Thus, when the high priest left the sanctuary that day, in type, there would be no more remembrance or thought of sin. Now let's look at it from another perspective.

The Casting of Lots

On the Day of Atonement, the Scripture states:

And he shall take of the congregation of the children of Israel two kids of the goats for a sin offering, and one ram for a burnt offering....And he shall take the two goats, and present them

before the LORD *at* **the door of the tabernacle of the congregation. And Aaron shall cast lots upon the two goats; one lot for the LORD, and the other lot for the scapegoat. And Aaron shall bring the goat upon which the LORD'S lot fell, and offer him** *for* **a sin offering.** (Lev. 16:7–9)

The Lord's Goat

The goat upon which the lot fell was called the Lord's goat. It was to be slain as a more unconventional sin offering for the people. Why was this goat specially identified as the Lord's goat? Because the priest was to bring his blood within the veil and sprinkle it before and upon the mercy seat. The blood was to also be sprinkled upon the altar of incense that was before the veil. This ritual provides full and final atonement for God's people.

In the sin offerings presented daily in the outer court by the regular priest, a substitute had been accepted in the sinner's stead, but the blood of the victim only provided pardon as it cleansed the heart of guilt. The sins still maintained a (temporary) presence as they were graven on the horns of the golden altar before God. The offerings restrain Him from destroying the penitent believers until they have obtained total victory and are made perfect through the final work of atonement, accomplished by way of blotting out the cumulative sins from the sanctuary.

Why is it that when we confess our sins, they are not blotted out immediately? God does not want sinners to remember their sins again. First, He takes them into the sanctuary through the blood of the sin offering, engraves them upon the horns of the altar. The sins are forgiven and pardoned. The psalmist speaks of this in the following way: **"Blessed is he whose transgression** *is* **forgiven,** *whose* **sin** *is* **covered"** (Lev. 32:1).

Though the sin is covered with blood, it does not mean the record of the sin is not there. For the record of sin to be blotted out and wiped away completely, something further must be done. Let us mention again that one of the most fundamental factors of the Christian life is conversion. Every professed Christian needs to experience the peace of mind that conversion brings. Repentance and conversion are among Peter's prerequisites for the blotting out of sins. **"Repent ye therefore, and be converted, that your sins may be blotted out, when the times of refreshing shall come from the presence of the Lord"** (Acts 3:19).

The blotting out of sins is another very important factor in the plan of salvation. We realize that people can never be fully satisfied and have unquestioned peace of mind until they know that every known sin has been confessed, forsaken, and forgiven. Then they can look forward to that day when the record of their sins will be permanently blotted out by the finger of God.

> As the books of record are opened in the judgment, the lives of all who have believed on Jesus come in review before God. Beginning with those who first lived upon the earth, our Advocate presents the cases of each successive generation, and closes with the living. Every name is mentioned, every case closely investigated. Names are accepted, names rejected. When any have sins remaining upon the books of record, unrepented of and unforgiven, their names will be blotted out of the book of life, and the record of their good deeds will be erased from the book of God's remembrance.... (White, *The Faith I Live By*, p. 212)

The Scapegoat

After conducting the ritual that cleansed the sanctuary, what did the high priest do?

> And when he hath made an end of reconciling the holy ***place***, and the tabernacle of the congregation, and the altar, he shall bring the live goat: And Aaron shall lay both his hands upon the head of the live goat, and confess over him all the iniquities of the children of Israel, and all their transgressions in all their sins, putting them upon the head of the goat, and shall send ***him*** away by the hand of a fit man into the wilderness: And the goat shall bear upon him all their iniquities unto a land not inhabited: and he shall let go the goat in the wilderness. (Lev. 16:20–22)

Please note that when the high priest came forth from the sanctuary, after sprinkling the blood of the Lord's goat on the mercy seat for the remission of Israel's sins, these sins were not placed upon the scapegoat in any propitiatory, atoning, or substitutionary sense. The Scripture distinctly declares that the atonement for the congregation of Israel had already been made when the high priest came out of the sanctuary.

The scapegoat's blood was not shed or taken into the sanctuary; it was not killed near the tabernacle; it was not placed upon the altar of sacrifice. For the life of every living thing is in the blood, so when the scapegoat died without shedding blood, it did not pour out or lay down its life for others.

It means its life was not offered as a substitution, but as a culprit. It died with its own blood on its head.

The sins that are brought out of the sanctuary on the Day of Atonement are placed on the scapegoat's head. These sins are the sins of repentant Israel, the people of God. The scapegoat carries away the sins into the wilderness and returns no more to the camp of Israel, thus separating the sins from the congregation forever. The man who led him away was required to wash himself and his clothing with water before returning to the camp (see v. 26).

Once the sun set and the Day of Atonement ended, God's people began, as it were, a fresh, new experience with Him. Their record was now a clean one; the atonement was completed. They were purged and cleansed from all sin, and so was the sanctuary.

In the antitype, as the high priest laid aside his pontifical dress and officiated in the white linen dress of a common priest, so Christ emptied Himself, took the form of a servant, and offered a sacrifice—Himself the priest, Himself the victim. The blood of the Son of God was symbolized by the blood of the sin offering.

Type and Antitype

Just as the high priest, on the Day of Atonement, first makes atonement with the ram of the sin offering for himself and his family, so Jesus, after His resurrection, appeared before God the Father, bearing human nature. **"Jesus saith unto her, Touch me not; for I am not yet ascended to my Father: but go to my brethren, and say unto them, I ascend unto my Father, and your Father; and *to* my God, and your God"** (John 20:17).

> Jesus refused to receive the homage of His people until He should know that His sacrifice had been accepted by the Father. He ascended to the heavenly courts, and from God Himself heard the assurance that His atonement for the sins of men had been ample, and through His blood all might gain eternal life.
>
> All power in Heaven and on earth was given to the Prince of Life, and He returned to His followers in a world of sin, that He might impart to them His power and glory. (White, *The Story of Jesus*, p. 160)

The earthly sanctuary was a type of the heavenly. Just as the earthly sanctuary had to be purified or cleansed by the blood of the sin offering, in a similar way the heavenly must be purified with the blood of a better sacrifice. The cleansing, both in parable and reality, was to be accomplished through the blood. The Bible says, *"It was* therefore necessary that the patterns of things in the heavens should be purified with these; but the heavenly things themselves with better sacrifices than these. For Christ is not entered into the holy places made with hands, *which are* the figures of the true; but into heaven itself, now to appear in the presence of God for us" (Heb. 9:23, 24).

Thus, when Jesus our High Priest finishes the cleansing of the heavenly sanctuary through blotting out the sins of His faithful people (having initially taken these sins upon Himself), Jesus will place the sins and their consequences upon Satan as the culprit. He will be declared guilty of all the evil that he has caused God's children to commit. The Word of God reveals the following:

"Whoso causeth the righteous to go astray in an evil way, he shall fall himself into his own pit: but the upright shall have good *things* in possession" (Prov. 28:10).

"He that diggeth a pit shall fall into it; and whoso breaketh an hedge, a serpent shall bite him" (Eccles. 10:8).

"Whoso diggeth a pit shall fall therein: and he that rolleth a stone, it will return upon him" (Prov. 26:27).

"His mischief shall return upon his own head, and his violent dealing shall come down upon his own pate" (Ps. 7:16).

Satan, as the antitypical scapegoat, does not bear these sins in any atoning sense. It is his own culpability for these transgressions that he bears. In the execution of God's judgment, he must bear the final penalty of the sins of God's people.

"And I saw an angel come down from heaven, having the key of the bottomless pit and a great chain in his hand. And he laid hold on the dragon, that old serpent, which is the Devil, and Satan, and bound him a thousand years, And cast him into the bottomless pit, and shut him up, and set a seal upon him, that he should deceive the nations no more" (Rev. 20:1–3).

As the scapegoat was sent away by the hand of a fit man into the wilderness, a land not inhabited, so at the second coming of Jesus Christ, an angel from heaven binds Satan and casts him into the bottomless pit, the abyss, the earth laid waste and depopulated. There he will be confined, or shut up, during the millennium. What happens after the millennium?

And they went up on the breadth of the earth, and compassed the camp of the saints about, and the beloved city: and fire came down from God out of heaven, and devoured them. And the devil that deceived them was cast into the lake of fire and brimstone, where

the beast and the false prophet *are*, and shall be tormented day and night forever and ever. (Rev. 20:9, 10).

The Day of Judgment

The Day of Atonement was also seen as a day of judgment for the people of God. The Scripture reveals the following: **"Also on the tenth day of this seventh month *there shall be* a day of atonement: it shall be an holy convocation unto you; and ye shall afflict your souls, and offer an offering made by fire unto the LORD...For whatsoever soul *it be* that shall not be afflicted in that same day, he shall be cut off from among his people"** (Lev. 23:27, 29).

Once the sun set and the Day of Atonement ended, God's people began, as it were, a fresh, new experience with Him.

We found that the Lord commanded that the person who did not observe this day must be cut off (separated) from among His people. Those who seek cleansing from sin, yet don't obey the command of God, show themselves unworthy of eternal life, practically sealing their destinies and closing their probation.

On the other hand, regarding those who sinned during the year, though they disobeyed and perhaps even forsook the Lord, if they heeded the command of God, observed this day, and sought pardon through the blood, were forgiven, accepted, and recognized as one of God's own. They were joined to the people of God.

This day's actions practically decided the life or death of someone. It truly was a day of judgment. To this day, Jews recognize this fact, for many of them use *Yom Kippur* ("Day of Atonement") and *Yom Hadin* ("Day of Judgment") interchangeably. Please note that to separate someone from the camp, an investigation was carried out to ascertain who did and didn't participated in personal soul affliction. The verdict was then passed upon those found guilty, while the execution of judgment came afterward—separation.

How does the atonement relate to the great antitype and judgment day? What does the Bible say about judgment day? Will Christians be judged? If so, when? In what kind of assurance should all Christians rejoice? This and many other questions will be addressed in the next chapter.

CHAPTER 6

Believers And Judgment

In this chapter, we shall discover whether God's people truly come to judgment or not. We are living in a time when people are unconcerned about His judgment, and many of those who profess faith in Christ believe they are immune from judgment altogether. They place strong emphasis on the following words: **"Verily, verily, I say unto you, He that heareth my word, and believeth on him that sent me, hath everlasting life, and shall not come into condemnation; but is passed from death unto life"** (John 5:24).

It is argued that the word "condemnation" in this verse means "judgment," which is technically true, to an extent. The Greek word used here is *krisis*, which is used by the King James Version in other verses:

Damnation: Matthew 23:33; Mark 3:29; John 5:29
Condemnation: John 3:19; John 5:24

Accusation: 2 Peter 2:11; Jude 9
Judgment: Matthew 5:21–22, 10:15; Mark 6:11; John 5:22; and others

How do we know which option is the right application? The Apostle Paul wrote:

> For what man knoweth the things of a man, save the spirit of man which is in him? Even so the things of God knoweth no man, but the Spirit of God. Now we have received, not the spirit of the world, but the spirit which is of God; that we might know the things that are freely given to us of God. Which things also we speak, not in the words which man's wisdom teacheth, but which the Holy Ghost teacheth; comparing spiritual things with spiritual. (1 Cor. 2:11–13)

Concerning the matter regarding whether or not believers come to Judgment, we have to humbly look at all the clear verses in Scripture which deal with judgment. First of all, we must take into consideration the differences between the meanings of the above options:

Damnation: state of being in hell as punishment after death
Condemnation: statement/expression of very strong, definite criticism/disapproval
Accusation: claim that someone has done something wrong or illegal
Judgment: act/process of investigating a matter by way of examination, verdict, and execution

Shall We Come to Judgment?

Now, having established this, our next and big question is, "What does the Scripture teach about judgment as it relates to believers?" We are told, "For God shall bring every work into judgment, with every secret thing, whether *it be* good, or whether *it be* evil" (Eccles. 12:14). Here the Scripture reveals that God will bring every secret thing, both good and bad, to judgment. Although the above text did not specify whether believers will be part of such judgment, let's compare other verses with the above text.

"I said in mine heart, God shall judge the righteous and the wicked: for *there is* a time there for every purpose and for every work" (Eccles. 3:17). Here it seems that no one will be exempted.

"For we must all appear before the judgment seat of Christ; that every one may receive the things *done* in *his* body, according to that he hath done, whether *it be* good or bad" (2 Cor. 5:10). Paul, similar to Solomon, states that no one will be exempted and that everybody will appear before the judgment seat of Christ. However, the next big question is, "To what kind of judgment will believers come?" Keep in mind that Ecclesiastes 12:14 includes both good and bad works. What does this suggest?

Each one of us is going to be weighed in the balance of God. The character we cultivate, the attitudes we assume today, are fixing our destiny for time and eternity. The choices we make and the deeds that result are all faithfully chronicled in the books of heaven, and it will be seen from the record whether our characters are after the order of obedience or lawlessness, which originated as rebellion in heaven. We are deciding today by our attitudes and character development whether we will be found wearing the white robes of righteousness or lost when Jesus returns.

Our indecision becomes decision in the wrong direction. Many will fail of entering the kingdom because they failed to make determined efforts to overcome their defects of character. Many, while expecting at some future time to overcome the problems in their lives, are approaching eternal loss. It is on this basis that the light of the first angel shines to a dying world.

> **And I saw another angel fly in the midst of heaven, having the everlasting gospel to preach unto them that dwell on the earth, and to every nation, and kindred, and tongue, and people, Saying with a loud voice, Fear God, and give glory to him; for the hour of his judgment is come: and worship him that made heaven, and earth, and the sea, and the fountains of waters.** (Rev. 14:6–7)

Through the first angel, men are called to fear, glorify, and worship God as the Creator of heaven and earth. The announcement **"The hour of his judgment is come"** suggests a process which already commenced.

This brings us to another interesting question: When does God's judgment actually commence for any given person—before death, or at death? The Holy Scripture says, **"and as it is appointed unto men once to die, but after this the judgment"** (Heb. 9:27). Paul categorically states that there will be judgment immediately after death. Another question is, "To what kind of judgment is he making reference?" And where will God's judgment take place—in heaven or in the graves? **"But the LORD shall endure for ever: he hath prepared his throne for judgment"** (Ps. 9:7).

Where is God's throne? The Bible says, **"We have such an high priest, who is set on the right hand of the throne of the Majesty in the heavens"**

(Heb. 8:1). God's throne is in heaven, and from here we are told, **"He shall judge the world in righteousness; he shall minister judgment to the people in uprightness"** (Ps. 9:8).

How does our case appear before God in judgment? Let's look at this following Bible text: **"Some men's sins are open beforehand, going before to judgment; and some *men* they follow after. Likewise also the good works *of some* are manifest beforehand; and they that are otherwise cannot be hid"** (1 Tim. 5:24, 25). Here we are told that in God's judgment, some people's sins will be open and precede beforehand to judgment, while for others their sins will follow after them to judgment.

Though all nations and people are to pass in judgment before God, they are divided into two camps: those whose sins precede to the judgment and those whose sins follow afterward.

Please note that in God's Word, we are told that God will examine the case of each individual with a close and searching scrutiny, as if there were not another being upon the earth.

Now let's look at it from this perspective. If judgment follows immediately after death, and some people's sins precede them to judgment, this suggests that certain people's cases are determined while they are still alive. Who falls into this category? Here is the testimony of the Scripture:

"For the time *is come* that judgment must begin at the house of God: and if *it* first *begin* at us, what shall the end *be* of them that obey not the gospel of God" (1 Peter 4:17)?

What does this imply? Those whose sins proceed first to the judgment are God's children; called by God's name; members of God's family; the church of our Lord Jesus Christ. This suggests that those whose sins follow after to the judgment are unbelievers. What kind of judgment are we talking about here? To better answer this, let's look at judgment in its three stages.

Stages of Judgment

First of all, there can be no judgment without a courtroom. A supreme court is the highest court within the hierarchy of many legal jurisdictions. Supreme courts typically function primarily as appellate courts, hearing appeals from the decisions of lower trial courts or intermediate-level appellate courts. In this case, the heavenly supreme court is the highest court in the universe. The supreme court of heaven shows divine justice as it's available for every believer. There are three stages of judgment:

1. **Investigative Judgment/Examination Trial**

2. Verdict Judgment/Condemnation or Vindication
3. Executive Judgment/Implementation of Court Order

Standard of Judgment

First of all, before we look at the three stages of judgment in detail, let's consider this: In our judicial procedures on earth, the usual purpose of a court trial is to determine whether a crime has been committed (a law broken). Only when a law has been violated can a person be found guilt. In God's judgment, there is a law or standard, and James makes it clear which law that is: "So speak ye, and so do, as they that shall be judged by the law of liberty" (James 2:12). In the previous verse, James mentioned two of the Ten Commandments: "For he that said, Do not commit adultery, said also, Do not kill. Now if thou commit no adultery, yet if thou kill, thou art become a transgressor of the law" (v. 11).

Obviously, God's Ten Commandments are the standard by which the lives of people will be judged. James, years after the Christian era began, emphasizes the obligation of the Christian to keep the law of the Ten Commandments—not merely one precept, but all of them. Therefore, what conclusion are we given by the wise man? "Let us hear the conclusion of the whole matter: Fear God, and keep his commandments: for this *is* the whole *duty* of man" (Eccles. 12:13).

What reason did Solomon give for urging all to fear God and keep His commandments? "For God shall bring every work into judgment, with every secret thing, whether *it be* good, or whether *it be* evil" (v. 14). Every individual must face judgment for deeds done in the body, whether good or bad. We should not forget that the standard of that judgment is the holy law of God, the Ten Commandments. Let's now look in detail at judgment in its three stages.

Investigative Judgment/Examination

The investigative judgment begins with a lawsuit, otherwise known as litigation. It begins when a complaint or petition is filed with the court. The litigant or plaintiff filed this case through his prosecuting attorney. The courts clerk stamps the court seal upon a summons, which is then served by the courts clerk on behalf of the plaintiff to the defendant, together with a copy of the complaint, which notifies the defendant of the nature of the accusation.

This service notifies the defendant that they are being sued and have a limited amount of time to reply. The defendant is required, through his attorney, to respond to the plaintiff's complaint. All the claims are examined, and the exhibits are carefully studied and properly investigated and analyzed. The defendant has one of three choices to make: admitting the allegation, denying it, or pleading a lack of sufficient evidence to admit.

Verdict Judgment

If the plaintiff is successful in proving his case to a logical conclusion, the case is ruled in favor of the plaintiff. If not, the case is ruled in favor of the defendant. The ruling is called a verdict. Please note that a verdict is one in which the jury makes a complete finding and single conclusion on all issues presented to it.

First, the jury finds the facts, as proved by the evidence, then applies the law as instructed by the court, then finally returns a verdict that settles the case. Therefore, the investigative phase of the judiciary process is concluded with the pronouncement of either condemnation or vindication.

In every trial, when the guilt of the defendant has been determined, there is a date set for a verdict. During this period of time, the evidence that has been produced in the trial is re-evaluated, then the sentence is determined and finally pronounced.

Executive Judgment

In the law, executive judgment is a court order granted to put in force a judgment of possession obtained by a plaintiff from a court verdict. This is the final stage of judgment where a court order is issued to enforce a verdict—the execution of a sentence. With this understanding comes our next question: When will God's executive judgment take place?

> **And Enoch also, the seventh from Adam, prophesied of these, saying, Behold, the Lord cometh with ten thousands of his saints, To execute judgment upon all, and to convince all that are ungodly among them of all their ungodly deeds which they have ungodly committed, and of all their hard *speeches* which ungodly sinners have spoken against him.** (Jude 14, 15)

The executive judgment takes place at the second coming of Christ. First, the saints are rewarded at the coming of Christ, the very beginning of the millennium reign. After the millennium, the wicked receive their recompense.

If you recall, we pointed out that the sins of every member of the household of God are opened beforehand in the judgment. Our question is, "How does our sin first get to the judgment?"

Adversary

Dear friends, I wish to let you know this important fact: there are spiritual enemies contending daily over our souls. To them, we are prizes they are trying to attain. Our adversary comes against every soul with legal papers concerning all our misdeeds. The Scripture gave an account of how Job's spiritual adversary wrote a book about him: **"Oh that one would hear me! behold, my desire *is, that* the Almighty would answer me, and *that* mine adversary had written a book"** (Job 31:35).

To which adversary was Job referring? Here is one of the clues the Bible gives: **"Be sober, be vigilant; because your adversary the devil, as a roaring lion, walketh about, seeking whom he may devour"** (1 Peter 5:8). Furthermore, the Scripture reveals that **"There was in a city a judge, who feared not God, neither regarded man: And there was a widow in that city; and she came unto him, saying, Avenge me of mine adversary"** (Luke 18:2, 3)

The adversary, in this context, is the enemy of the human soul—Satan. In addition, he charges his following agencies to misrepresent, tempt, and destroy the people of God. Those who have decided to do the will of God will understand by experience that they have adversaries who are controlled by a power from beneath. Such adversaries beset Christ at every step—how constantly and determinedly no human being can ever know. Christ's disciples, like their Master, are followed by continual temptation.

Day by day, Satan and his agents are laying snares to overthrow God's people. They try to keep an accurate record of the sins of God's people. With these legal documents, they accuse us before God. That's why the Bible says, **"for the accuser of our brethren is cast down, which accused them before our God day and night"** (Rev. 12:10). **"And he shewed me Joshua the high priest standing before the angel of the LORD, and Satan standing at his right hand to resist him. And the LORD said unto Satan, the LORD rebuke thee, O Satan; even the LORD that hath chosen Jerusalem rebuke thee: *is* not this a brand plucked out of the fire"** (Zech. 3:1, 2)?

Joshua here represents the people of God, and Satan, pointing to their filthy garments, claims them as his property over which he has a right to exercise his cruel power. However, these very ones have employed the hours of probation to confess their sins with contrition of soul and put them away, and Jesus has written pardon upon their names. This is what our sins coming beforehand to the judgment looks like.

The Two Attorneys

Please note that within the context of judgment, there are always two attorneys: the prosecuting attorney and the defense attorney. In God's judgment, Satan is the prosecuting attorney and Jesus is the defense attorney. The Bible says, "My little children, these things write I unto you, that ye sin not. And if any man sin, we have an advocate with the Father, Jesus Christ the righteous" (1 John 2:1).

The term "advocate" in Greek is *parakletos*, which means "intercessor," "consoler," or "comforter." "Advocate" and "intercessor" are synonymous with "attorney." Jesus is the believer's attorney. The Holy Spirit is the heavenly court clerk who stamps the court seal upon every summons from the supreme court of the universe. He also serves us a copy of the summons containing Satan's complaints and claims against us before the heavenly supreme court. Please note that God's summons to our soul is a call for us to complete surrender our lives to His lordship.

The Holy Spirit reveals to us all our sinfulness, which is the basis of Satan's litigation against us. He opens before our minds the legal documents containing all our misdeeds, put together by our adversary the devil, for the purpose of claiming us as his lawful captives. The wicked one then stands on the Word of God, which says, "He that committeth sin is of the devil; for the devil sinneth from the beginning" (1 John 3:8).

Pointing to all our shortcomings, he takes accurate records of every sin he has caused us to commit, then puts together a solid legal case against us, written in a book (see Job 31:35).

The adversary here is the devil, but one of the first things the Holy Spirit does, while trying to deliver us from the hand of the strong man, is bring contrition to our hearts and brokenness of spirit, before He then reveals our ingratitude that has slighted and grieved the Savior, thus bringing us in contrition to the foot of the cross.

The Holy Spirit also imparts repentance to us and convinces us to seek the service of a defense attorney—our Advocate Jesus. He takes up all the records of allegation leveled against us by Satan and his demonic agents, ready to help us in our weakness. He presents it to Christ in a groan that cannot be refuted. Speaking of this, the Bible says:

Likewise the Spirit also helpeth our infirmities: for we know not what we should pray for as we ought: but the Spirit itself maketh intercession for us with groanings which cannot be uttered. And he that searcheth the hearts knoweth what is the mind of the

Spirit, because he maketh intercession for the saints according to the will of God. (Rom. 8:26, 27)

By the reason of this satanic accusation, the sins of all the believers now go beforehand to an investigative judgment. We cannot step into God's hallowed chambers without adequate counsel. Therefore, we need an advocate, One willing to go for us to plead our cases. In our absence, the case is thoroughly deliberated by a well-known Attorney who, by His intercessory defense, fosters an outcome of "Not Guilty" by reason of forgiveness. Thus, we are vindicated and not condemned. The Scripture says, **"For He has rescued us from the dominion of darkness and brought us into the Kingdom of the Son He loves, in whom we have redemption, the forgiveness of sins"** (Col. 1:13, 14, NIV).

We have clearly seen in both the Old and New Testaments that we all must appear before God's judgment seat to have our actions evaluated, whether they are good or evil. Hence, when John 5:24 speaks of believers not coming into judgment, it is condemnation to which John is referring, not examination. We have already seen Christ's statement about our having to give an account in the judgment for the following reason: **"But I say unto you, That every idle word that men shall speak, they shall give account thereof in the day of judgment. For by thy words thou shalt be justified, and by thy words thou shalt be condemned"** (Matt. 12:36, 37).

Whether we believe it or not, whether we like it or not, whether we profess to be Christians or not, we must all appear before the judgment seat of God. God has no favorites. Anyone who is summoned by the court in heaven, must appear. **"So then every one of us shall give account of himself to God"** (Rom. 14:12).

The decision of heaven's court will be irrevocable, for there is no higher court of appeal. It will forever seal the destiny of every person. However, before a verdict can be given or sentence passed, there must be a judgment of examination, trial, or investigation. That is a key component to the message of the first angel: **"Fear God, and give glory to him; for the hour of his judgment is come: and worship him that made heaven, and earth, and the sea, and the fountains of waters"** (Rev. 14:7). This message does not say that God's judgment *will* come. Rather, it *is* come—the judgment has already begun.

Don't get me wrong. In our study, we've established the fact that the judgment of the great day is an event certain to take place: **"He hath appointed a day, in the which he will judge the world in righteousness by *that* man whom he hath ordained"** (Acts 17:31). Therefore, what God has appointed is sure to come: **"Some men's sins are open beforehand, going before to judgment; and some other [men] theirs follow after"** (1 Tim. 5:24). This reference suggests a pre-advent judgment—a trial that closes with a verdict judgment. Now what does the Bible say about our condition when we are dead?

> **For the living know that they shall die: but the dead know not any thing, neither have they any more a reward; for the memory of them is forgotten. Also their love, and their hatred, and their envy, is now perished; neither have they any more a portion forever in any** *thing* **that is done under the sun.... Whatsoever thy hand findeth to do, do** *it* **with thy might; for** *there is* **no work, nor device, nor knowledge, nor wisdom, in the grave, whither thou goest.** (Eccles. 9:5, 6, 10)

The Word of God has made it very clear that the dead cannot do anything to correct their past mistakes, faults, or sinful records in heaven. Thus, as soon as someone dies, at that moment, that person's guarding angel who keeps record of one's life returns back to God and presents the record. A person may live a fairly good life on earth without Christ, but what happens after death? The court commences immediately as the Father takes His seat to make the final verdict. Satan comes forward with his legal document to claim the body of the dead. The Bible says, **"Yet Michael the archangel, when contending with the devil he disputed about the body of Moses, durst not bring against him a railing accusation, but said, The Lord rebuke thee"** (Jude 1:9).

The devil presents his accusation, and the Father turns to Jesus to know what He would say about the dead person. If that person had not accepted Christ before death, Christ would respond this way: "I did everything I could that this person might be saved. Father, I gave my life for this young one. Father, I died on Calvary. What more could I have done? However, this person would not accept my sacrifice or accept me as a personal Lord and Savior. Therefore, I cannot cover this person's sins with my blood." Slowly but surely, God the Father says, "Put this name in the book of death."

However, if this person had accepted Jesus as a personal Lord and Savior, Christ would say, "I cover this person's sins with my blood." Slowly but surely, God the Father would say, "Retain this name in the book of life." This is not the end of the story. The Bible says, **"For the Lord himself shall descend from heaven with a shout, with the voice of the archangel,** and with the trump of God: and the dead in Christ shall rise first: Then we which are alive [and] remain shall be caught up together with them in the clouds, to meet the Lord in the air: and so shall we ever be with the Lord" (1 Thess. 4:16, 17).

In the first resurrection, when Jesus returns to the earth the second time, only those whose names are written in the Lamb's book of life will be raised. What about the wicked? "But the rest of the dead lived not again until the thousand years were finished. This *is* the first resurrection. Blessed and holy *is* he that hath part in the first resurrection: on such the second death hath no power, but they shall be priests of God and of Christ, and shall reign with him a thousand years" (Rev. 20:5, 6).

At the end of the thousand years, Jesus descends to the earth, and the second resurrection takes place. The Bible says, "And I saw the dead, small and great, stand before God; and the books were opened: and another book was opened, which is *the book* of life: and the dead were judged out of those things which were written in the books, according to their works.... And whosoever was not found written in the book of life was cast into the lake of fire" (vs. 12, 15).

With the judgment of the wicked being a distinct and separate work, it takes place at a later period. Speaking of this, Paul wrote, "Do ye not know that the saints shall judge the world? and if the world shall be judged by you, are ye unworthy to judge the smallest matters? Know ye not that we shall judge angels? how much more things that pertain to this life" (1 Cor. 6:2, 3)?

He tells us that the saints will judge not only the earth, but angels; yet the righteous are themselves to pass the test of the judgment. Thus, it follows that the judgment must pass upon the righteous before they can sit in judgment of the wicked. This is a very important proposition, and we know that it is truthful from the express testimony of the Scriptures:

> *The decision of heaven's court will be irrevocable, for there is no higher court of appeal. It will forever seal the destiny of every person.*

> And I saw thrones, and they sat upon them, and judgment was given unto them: and *I saw* the souls of them that were beheaded for the witness of Jesus, and for the word of God, and which had not worshipped the beast, neither his image, neither had received

> *his* **mark upon their foreheads, or in their hands; and they lived and reigned with Christ a thousand years.** (Rev. 20:4)

> **I beheld, and the same horn made war with the saints, and prevailed against them; Until the Ancient of days came, and judgment was given to the saints of the most High; and the time came that the saints possessed the kingdom.** (Dan. 7:21, 22)

Here is the exalted work of the saints in the millennium reign of Christ. They are to take part in the examination of the cases of all wicked people and fallen angels. However, this is not to be until they have been changed to immortality and exalted to thrones of glory. They do not, therefore, have their cases decided at the same time as the wicked do. We believe that the reader will acknowledge the justice of this reasoning. **"To execute upon them the judgment written: this honour have all his saints. Praise ye the LORD"** (Ps. 149:9).

CHAPTER 7

The Glorious Heavenly Court

In this chapter, we will take a spectacular journey to God's glorious, heavenly court and answer some questions. In the Holy Scriptures, we are told that the earthly sanctuary built by Moses was patterned after the heavenly sanctuary. In our study so far, we've been able to prove that there is indeed a heavenly temple, but let's ask a significant question: Do the earthly and heavenly sanctuaries match exactly?

"Neither by the blood of goats and calves, but by his own blood he entered in once into the holy place, having obtained eternal redemption for us" (Heb. 9:12). The Greek term for "holy place" here is *ta hagia*, a plural term which literally means "holies" (or "holy places"). It is evident that Paul is referring to the temple as a whole (a multi-room unit).

Seen by John in Heaven

"And the temple of God was opened in heaven, and there was seen in his temple the ark of his testament: and there were lightnings, and

voices, and thunderings, and an earthquake, and great hail" (Rev. 11:19). John, while on the island of Patmos, was taken to heaven in vision and shown a temple with the ark of God in it. what was the ark? It was the article of furniture in the Most Holy Place. Did you notice we were told in Exodus that the sanctuary is a place where God dwells—in other words, His throne room. What other things were seen in this temple in heaven?

"And out of the throne proceeded lightnings and thunderings and voices: and *there were* seven lamps of fire burning before the throne, which are the seven Spirits of God" (Rev. 4:5). John saw seven lamps of fire burning before the throne. Here is the antitype of the golden candlestick of the earthly sanctuary, with its seven branches. What other things did he see in the temple above?

"And another angel came and stood at the altar, having a golden censer; and there was given unto him much incense, that he should offer *it* with the prayers of all saints upon the golden altar which was before the throne" (Rev. 8:3). John also saw the altar of incense and a censer in heaven. No doubt you can see that what John was describing here was the sanctuary, for it had furniture that only belonged to the sanctuary. He mentioned the essential articles of furniture. What else do we need? Moses says he made the sanctuary after the pattern shown him.

The book of Hebrews says plainly that the pattern was the true sanctuary that is heaven, and John completes the chain of evidence by saying that he actually saw it there. From his description of the various articles, we see the furniture of the two apartments clearly defined, in harmony with the plan of the earthly tabernacle built by Moses. Our next big question is this: Are there also three sections in the sanctuary above? If yes, can it be proven?

Heavenly Outer Court

> Now the cherubims stood on the right side of the house, when the man went in; and the cloud filled the inner court. Then the glory of the LORD went up from the cherub, *and stood* over the threshold of the house; and the house was filled with the cloud, and the court was full of the brightness of the LORD'S glory. And the sound of the cherubims' wings *was heard even to the outer court*, as the voice of the Almighty God when he speaketh. (Ezek. 10:3–5, emphasis mine)

> And the temple was filled with smoke from the glory of God, and from his power; and no man was able to enter into the temple, till the seven plagues of the seven angels were fulfilled. (Rev. 15:8)

Both prophets used some similar imagery, though Ezekiel made reference to an outer court. The Scripture confirms there was an outer court in heaven, because when the court of the sanctuary was filled with cloud, smoke, and the brightness of God's glory, nobody was seen in the sanctuary, so all the angels were outside the temple. We are told that the sound within was heard outside the temple as the voice of the Almighty. Though the immediate outer court in heaven has no altar of sacrifice or laver, it is interesting to note that the entire universe is an outer court to God's temple, for these are the territories of His dominion sovereignty.

Our own planet earth is but an atom in the vast expanse over which God presides, yet this little fallen world—the one lost sheep—is more precious in His sight than are the ninety and nine that went not astray from the fold. Christ, the loved Commander in the heavenly courts, in other to save the one lost world, stooped from His high estate, laid aside the glory that He had with the Father, and came to our sin-cursed world.

The altar of sacrifice and laver of water outside the earthly sanctuary represent the sacrifice of Jesus on the cross of Calvary for our little lost world. The altar served to present Jesus Christ, the Lamb of God, who offered Himself to die for us as our burnt offering, while the laver points to Christ's baptism and ability to clean us and makes us acceptable before the very presence of our great God. Is there a veil or door separating the Holy Place from the Most Holy Place in the heavenly sanctuary?

Naos—The Inner Shrine

> "And the temple of God was opened in heaven, and there was seen in his temple the ark of his testament: and there were lightnings, and voices, and thunderings, and an earthquake, and great hail" (Rev. 11:19). "And after that I looked, and, behold, the temple of the tabernacle of the testimony in heaven was opened" (Rev. 15:5).

Please note, the Bible texts we read said the temple in heaven was opened. In Greek, there are two words for "temple," and the first word is *hieron*, which refers to the totality of the temple, or the whole building. However, that is not the word that is used here in Revelation. The word that is used here is *naos*, which alludes to the inner shrine of the temple—the Most Holy Place. Another piece of evidence confirming that it is the Most Holy Place is the reference to the ark of God's testimony or testament.

Does the following verse suggest that Christ's flesh is the veil or door that demarcates the holy place from the most holy place? **"By a new and living way, which he hath consecrated for us, through the veil, that is to say, his flesh"** (Heb. 10:20). The context in which this verse is set recommends a broader view. It is more appropriate to conclude that we have access to God because of Jesus' humanity, through which He became our propitiatory sacrifice and representative High Priest.

The mercy seat, upon which the glory of God rested in the holiest of all, is opened to all who accept Christ as the propitiation for sin, and through its medium, they are brought into fellowship with God. The veil is rent, the partition walls are broken down, and the handwriting of ordinances are cancelled. By virtue of His blood, the enmity is abolished. How many thrones are in God's temple?

The Thrones in the Temple

"I beheld till the thrones were cast down, and the Ancient of days did sit, whose garment *was* white as snow, and the hair of his head like the pure wool: his throne *was like* the fiery flame, *and* his wheels *as* burning fire" (Dan. 7:9). God's abode is not an empty room; inside that temple is the most majestic throne one could imagine. Did you notice the word used by Daniel for "throne" is plural, indicating more than one throne? In God's temple, you find the thrones of God and Christ.

Throne of the Father

The throne of the Father is the throne of the universe. David, speaking of this throne, says, **"The LORD hath prepared his throne in the heavens; and his kingdom ruleth over all"** (Ps. 103:19). Daniel, speaking of the Ancient of days, the Eternal Father, says that **"A fiery stream issued and came forth from before him: thousand thousands ministered unto him, and ten thousand times ten thousand stood before him"** (Dan. 7:10).

What is the throne of Christ called?

Throne of Christ

"Let us therefore come boldly unto the throne of grace, that we may obtain mercy, and find grace to help in time of need" (Heb. 4:16). The throne of Christ is called the throne of grace. The existence of a throne supposes the existence of a kingdom. The throne of grace represents the kingdom of grace. When the sacred Scriptures speak of heavenly thrones, heavenly kingdoms are meant. What article of furniture in the earthly sanctuary symbolizes the throne of grace? **"And there I will meet with thee, and I will commune with thee from above the mercy seat, from between the two cherubims which *are* upon the ark of the testimony"** (Exod. 25:22).

There is a very beautiful, practical lesson connected with the mercy seat. The Bible says, **"Being justified freely by his grace through the redemption that is in Christ Jesus: Whom God hath set forth *to be* a propitiation through faith in his blood, to declare his righteousness for the remission of sins that are past, through the forbearance of God"** (Rom. 3:24, 25).

The Greek word that is translated "propitiation" is *hilasterion*, and it means "mercy seat." In fact, this is the same word which is translated "mercyseat" in Hebrews 9:5. Therefore, we see that Jesus Christ is God's mercy seat. In Him, mercy and truth embraced each other with the loving arms of peace and righteousness. In Christ, God is dispensing mercy towards the children of humanity.

The Mercy Seat

Harkening back to Hebrew 4:16, there is a throne of mercy to which every soul can come in time of need. It would be useless to come before any throne for favor if that throne had no occupant. The throne of grace, therefore, supposes there is the King of grace.

If there is a king, He must have subjects, and laws to govern those subjects. Then, while in this state, as people receive grace and favor from God, they are in the kingdom of grace. The next question is, "Who is this king whose throne is between the cherub, and who are His subjects? **"The LORD reigneth; let the people tremble: he sitteth *between* the cherubims; let the earth be moved"** (Ps. 99:1). **"And Hezekiah prayed unto the LORD, saying, O LORD of hosts, God of Israel, that dwellest *between* the cherubims, thou *art* the God, *even* thou alone, of all the kingdoms of the earth: thou hast made heaven and earth"** (Isa. 37:15, 16). **"O Shepherd of Israel.... thou that dwellest *between* the cherubims, shine forth"** (Ps. 80:1).

We are told that the king whose seat is between the cherubim is the Lord of hosts, the God and Shepherd of Israel. Who in the Scriptures do we refer to as the Good Shepherd? It's no other than Jesus. He said:

> I am the good shepherd: the good shepherd giveth his life for the sheep.... I am the good shepherd, and know my *sheep*, and am

> known of mine. As the Father knoweth me, even so know I the Father: and I lay down my life for the sheep. And other sheep I have, which are not of this fold: them also I must bring, and they shall hear my voice; and there shall be one fold, *and* one shepherd. (John 10:11, 14–16)

Jesus is the king whose throne is between the cherubim, while the church—spiritual Israel—is the subject of His kingdom. The two lovely cherubs, one on each side of the ark, stood with their wings outstretched above it, touching each other above the head of Jesus as He stood before the mercy seat. Their faces were turned toward each other, and they looked downward to the ark, representing the entire angelic host, looking with interest at the law of God.

Between the cherubim was a golden censer, and as the prayers of the saints, offered in faith, came up to Jesus, and as He presented them to His Father, a cloud of fragrance arose from the incense upward to the Father's throne.

Our crucified Lord is pleading for us in the presence of the Father while sitting on the throne of grace. The Lamb slain is our only hope. Our faith looks up to Him, grasps Him as the One who can save to the uttermost, and the fragrance of the all-sufficient offering is accepted by the Father. Christ's glory is concerned with our success. He has a common interest in all humanity. He is our sympathizing Savior. Is Christ entitled only to the kingdom of grace, or has the Father also given Him another kingdom? If yes, what kingdom is that? And what throne would that be? **"When the Son of man shall come in his glory, and all the holy angels with him, then shall he sit upon the throne of his glory"** (Matt. 25:31).

The kingdom of grace is God's plan to save people by grace. It was established as early as mercy and grace were offered to fallen humanity. Adam, Abel, Noah, Abraham, and Moses were as legitimately the subjects of the kingdom of grace as the apostles and martyrs of Jesus were, or as the followers of Christ are now.

Our own planet earth is but an atom in the vast expanse over which God presides, yet this little fallen world—the one lost sheep—is more precious in His sight than are the ninety and nine that went not astray from the fold.

Kingdom of Glory

The kingdom of glory is future. In connection with its establishment will be the second coming of Christ in power and great glory, to raise the righteous. These, all immortal, will be eternal subjects of the kingdom of glory. In Paul's most solemn charge to Timothy, he associates the coming of Christ and the last judgment with the immortal kingdom. **"I charge *thee therefore* before God, and the Lord Jesus Christ, who shall judge the quick and the dead at his appearing and his kingdom; Preach the word; be instant in season, out of season; reprove, rebuke, exhort with all longsuffering and doctrine"** (2 Tim. 4:1, 2). This kingdom will be God's arrangement to glorify and reward the immortal righteous who are saved from every nation, tongue, and people during the ages of human probation.

The kingdom of grace and the kingdom of glory are closely related to each other. The former was established to prepare subjects for the latter. They span the ages from the fall, when the plan of redemption was instituted, embracing the eternal future. Two conditions of the people of God are expressed by the phrase "kingdom of heaven" so frequently used in the New Testament. Sometimes it expresses their present condition in this world, and sometimes their future condition in the world to come.

The Scriptures distinctly speak of two thrones. One is the throne of the Father; the other is the throne of the Son. Christ first sits on the throne of the Father to reign in connection with Him in the kingdom of grace until human probation shall close. He will then reign upon His throne forever, in the kingdom of glory. In these emphatic words, Christ addresses the church:

"To him that overcometh will I grant to sit with me in my throne, even as I also overcame, and am set down with my Father in his throne" (Rev. 3:21). In the kingdom of God, the crown and throne are tokens of a condition attained through the grace of our Lord Jesus Christ. The Bible says, **"And he that overcometh, and keepeth My works unto the end, to him will I give power over the nations"** (Rev. 2:26).

The Location of God's Throne

Does God's throne have a geographical location in the heavenly Sanctuary? The Bible says, **"And there I will meet with thee, and I will commune with thee from above the mercy seat, from between the two cherubims which *are* upon the ark of the testimony, of all *things* which I will give thee in commandment unto the children of Israel"** (Exod.

25:22). Here we are told that God communes with His people from above the mercy seat. Note the mercy seat is in between the cherubs. Hence, the position of the throne of Jehovah God the Father is situated above the mercy seat, but when communicating, God stoops low and speaks in between the mercy seat.

Now let's compare this with the heavenly reality. Here is what the Bible says: **"Then I looked, and, behold, in the firmament that was above the head of the cherubims there appeared over them as it were a sapphire stone, as the appearance of the likeness of a throne"** (Ezek. 10:1).

> **[A]nd upon the likeness of the throne *was* the likeness as the appearance of a man above upon it. And I saw as the colour of amber, as the appearance of fire round about within it, from the appearance of his loins even upward, and from the appearance of his loins even downward, I saw as it were the appearance of fire, and it had brightness round about. As the appearance of the bow that is in the cloud in the day of rain, so *was* the appearance of the brightness round about. This [was] the appearance of the likeness of the glory of the LORD. And when I saw [it], I fell upon my face, and I heard a voice of one that spake.** (Ezek. 1:26–28)

The prophet Ezekiel was describing the position of the throne of Jehovah God the Father in the heavenly sanctuary. He stated that the throne was seen above the cherubim, so the cherubim were below the throne, thus implying that the mercy seat that was between the cherubim was also below the throne of the Most High God. Isaiah states, **"In the year that king Uzziah died I saw also the Lord sitting upon a throne, high and lifted up, and his train filled the temple"** (Isa. 6:1).

When God was about to send Isaiah with a message to His people, He first permitted the prophet to look in vision into the Holy of holies within the sanctuary. Suddenly the gate and inner veil of the temple seemed to be uplifted or withdrawn, and he was permitted to gaze within, upon the Holy of holies, where even the prophet's feet might not enter.

There rose before him a vision of Jehovah sitting upon a throne, high and lifted up, while the train of His glory filled the temple. The description here also confirms the position of God's throne in the temple. His throne is high above, while every other thing in the sanctuary is below. Further describing God's dwelling, the Bible says, **"Now unto the King eternal, immortal, invisible, the only wise God…Who only hath immortality, dwelling in the light which no man can approach unto; whom no man**

hath seen, nor can see: to whom *be* **honour and power everlasting. Amen"** (1 Tim. 1:17; 6:16).

We are told that God is invisible and dwells in a light unapproachable. His throne is far above the cherubim in the Most Holy Place of the heavenly court. The cherubim that are bowing and looking downward, not upward, point to how all the angels bow in holy reverence before God, for none can look at His face. Our next important question is, "Who alone has seen God?"

"No man hath seen God at any time; the only begotten Son, which is in the bosom of the Father, he hath declared *him*" (John 1:18).

No eyes have ever seen God, except Christ's, the Only Begotten of the Father. It is only He who can approach the exceeding bright light which enshrouded the Father and be shut in by that glorious light. While God the Father remains invisible, Jesus is the only visible Being seen sitting on the throne in the heavenly sanctuary. Why? Because He is **"the image of the invisible God…For in him dwelleth all the fulness of the Godhead bodily"** (Col. 1:15; 2:9).

The Angels in the Temple

Having described God's throne and its position in the Most Holy Place of the heavenly sanctuary, as well as the throne of grace, our attention is next drawn to the position of the angels. Describing Satan's rebellion in heaven, the Bible says:

> **How art thou fallen from heaven, O Lucifer, son of the morning?** *how* **art thou cut down to the ground, which didst weaken the nations! For thou hast said in thine heart, I will ascend into heaven, I will exalt my throne above the stars of God: I will sit also upon the mount of the congregation, in the sides of the north: I will ascend above the heights of the clouds; I will be like the most High.** (Isa. 14:12–14)

From Isaiah's testimony, we notice that the throne of God is built on the top of the mountain of God's congregation—in other words, God's temple. The throne is located above the heights of the cloud in the mount of congregation. It is exalted above the stars of God. It was Satan's ambition to overthrow God and ascend to the top of the mount, on the side of the north, sit on God's throne, and be as God.

Please take note that in the earthly pattern of the heavenly sanctuary, the only beings recorded to have access to the Most Holy Place, besides

God and the high priest, are the cherubim. However, they were not at the top of the mount of congregation where the throne of God is, but rather beneath, around the mercy seat or, more specifically, the throne of grace.

In other words, it was designed to show how Jesus was surrounded by the host of angels. That was why the statues of the cherubim were graven at the two ends of the ark of the covenant in the earthly pattern. Is God's throne mobile? Is the presence of God confined to one place in the heavenly sanctuary?

The human pen cannot adequately portray the glory and solemnity of the Most Holy Place of the heavenly court, but the Bible gives us an accurate account. **"I beheld till the thrones were cast down, and the Ancient of days did sit, whose garment *was* white as snow, and the hair of his head like the pure wool: his throne *was like* the fiery flame, *and* his wheels *as* burning fire. A fiery stream issued and came forth from before him"** (Dan. 7:9, 10).

This is a very intriguing expression. Daniel said he beheld until the thrones were "cast down," from the Hebrew *remah*, which means "to be placed" or "re-arrangement." These phrases suggest a movement of the throne of God. The reference to the throne is plural, indicating that more than one throne was set forth. Since God's throne is originally set above the mercy seat, we are told in God's Word that the throne of the mercy seat is situated in between the covering cherubim, above the ark of the covenant in the Most Holy Place of the heavenly Sanctuary. It is also evident that besides these thrones were other, lesser thrones placed in position. Is the throne of Christ confined to one place?

The Mercy Seat Is Also Mobile

> **Then the glory of the LORD went up from the cherub, *and stood* over the threshold of the house; and the house was filled with the cloud, and the court was full of the brightness of the LORD'S glory.... Then the glory of the LORD departed from off the threshold of the house, and stood over the cherubims. And the cherubims lifted up their wings, and mounted up from the earth in my sight: when they went out, the wheels also *were* beside them, and *every one* stood at the door of the east gate of the LORD'S house; and the glory of the God of Israel *was* over them above.** (Ezek. 10:4, 18, 19)

The above passage from Daniel 7 shows that the throne of God has wheels and can move from one place to another, while in the book of

Ezekiel, we see the presence of Christ also moves within the temple to the threshold of the house.

The Presence of God

God is omnipresent, meaning He is present at all times and in all places. Though God's presence is everywhere, the Bible also speaks of His presence in certain locations, such as in the sanctuary. From the symbolic services of the earthly sanctuary, where does the priest encounter the presence of God?

> And he shall bring the bullock unto the door of the tabernacle of the congregation before the LORD; and shall lay his hand upon the bullock's head, and kill the bullock before the LORD. And the priest that is anointed shall take of the bullock's blood, and bring it to the tabernacle of the congregation: And the priest shall dip his finger in the blood, and sprinkle of the blood seven times before the LORD, before the vail of the sanctuary. And the priest shall put *some* of the blood upon the horns of the altar of sweet incense before the LORD, which *is* in the tabernacle of the congregation. (Lev. 4:4–7)

> In the tabernacle of the congregation without the vail, which *is* before the testimony, Aaron and his sons shall order it from evening to morning before the LORD: *it shall be* a statute for ever unto their generations on the behalf of the children of Israel. (Exod. 27:21)

In the above verses, we see that the presence of God is in each apartment of the sanctuary. Whoever is in these places is actually before the Lord. The priest ministering in the outer court is actually in the presence of God, and when before the veil and the altar of incense in the Holy Place, he is also in the presence of God. This phenomenon is not confined to the Most Holy Place. In the outer court, he is close; in the Holy Place, he is closer; but he is closest to God in the Most Holy Place.

Anointing and Consecration

Before any priest could take up his calling, he had to go through a solemn ritual which lasted for seven days. The instructions given by God began with this statement: "And this *is* the thing that thou shalt do unto them to hallow them, to minister unto me in the priest's office" (Exod. 29:1). "Hallow" means "to set something or someone apart" for a particular service. What follows is an act of consecration for service: "And thou shalt anoint Aaron and his sons, and consecrate them, that *they* may minister unto me in the priest's office" (Exod. 30:30).

When the sanctuary was made and its parts were all put together, the following command came to Moses:

> Take Aaron and his sons with him, and the garments, and the anointing oil, and a bullock for the sin offering, and two rams, and a basket of unleavened bread; And gather thou all the congregation together unto the door of the tabernacle of the congregation. And Moses did as the LORD commanded him; and the assembly was gathered together unto the door of the tabernacle of the congregation. And Moses said unto the congregation, This *is* the thing which the LORD commanded to be done. (Lev. 8:2–5)

Moses then brought his brother Aaron and his sons and washed them in the laver. He clothed them with the sacred robes in which they were to minister in the sanctuary. Following this part of the ceremony, "Moses took the anointing oil, and anointed the tabernacle and all that *was* therein, and sanctified them. And he sprinkled thereof upon the altar seven times, and anointed the altar and all his vessels, both the laver and his foot, to sanctify them. And he poured of the anointing oil upon Aaron's head, and anointed him, to sanctify him" (v. 10–12).

Aaron's sons also were to be anointed with this holy oil. The Scripture says:

> And thou shalt put upon Aaron the holy garments, and anoint him, and sanctify him; that he may minister unto me in the priest's office. And thou shalt bring his sons, and clothe them with coats: And thou shalt anoint them, as thou didst anoint their father, that they may minister unto me in the priest's office: for their anointing shall surely be an everlasting priesthood throughout their generations. (Exod. 40:13–15)

The Scripture says the following regarding the thoroughness with which this anointing with the holy oil was actually performed: "It is like the precious ointment upon the head, that ran down upon the beard, *even* Aaron's beard: that went down to the skirts of his garments" (Ps. 133:2). It was a most complete service which Moses performed upon his brother when he anointed him with the holy oil, in order that Aaron might be consecrated to the sacred and solemn work which was committed to him as the high priest of the earthly sanctuary. This holy oil was used for the purpose of dedicating the sanctuary and its vessels of service, as well as for the consecration of the priests to their ministry. This inaugural consecration service lasted seven days. **"And ye shall not go out of the door of the tabernacle of the congregation *in* seven days, until the days of your consecration be at an end: for seven days shall he consecrate you"** (Lev. 8:33).

None who were to take part in the service of the sanctuary were permitted to perform any labor during this time of inauguration and consecration. **"Therefore shall ye abide *at* the door of the tabernacle of the congregation day and night seven days, and keep the charge of the LORD, that ye die not: for so I am commanded"** (v. 35). What a solemn and sacred service this must have been! To question or minimize its value meant certain death. What other services were required in this inauguration?

> **Then shalt thou kill the ram, and take of his blood, and put it upon the tip of the right ear of Aaron, and upon the tip of the right ear of his sons, and upon the thumb of their right hand, and upon the great toe of their right foot, and sprinkle the blood upon the altar round about.... And thou shalt take the ram of the consecration, and seethe his flesh in the holy place.** (Exod. 29:20, 31)

The ceremony commences at the entrance of the tabernacle within the courtyard. At the killing of the ram, the blood is fetched and applied to the tips of Aaron's right ear, his sons' right ears, the thumbs of their right hands, and the great toes of their right feet. Some blood is also sprinkled upon the brazen altar. The next ritual takes place in the Holy Place. The consecrated ram's flesh is inside and seethed. **"And Aaron and his sons shall eat the flesh of the ram, and the bread that *is* in the basket, *by* the door of the tabernacle of the congregation"** (v. 32).

Please note the door of the tabernacle of the congregation spoken of in this context is the entrance door to the Holy Place. This was the installation ceremony of these men who were set apart for the service of God. How did this type meet its fulfillment in Christ's ministry? Before the Savior can begin His ministry as our High Priest, the heavenly sanctuary must be dedicated and anointed, and He must be consecrated to His high priesthood. This antitypical fulfillment is foretold by the Word of God. Four key events were involved in the dedication and anointing of the sanctuary and priesthood.

1. The washing and clothing of the priest and high priest
2. The anointing of the tabernacle and the priest
3. The blood ritual and the seething of the flesh in the Holy Place
4. The eating of the flesh of the ram at the door of the tabernacle

The Washing and Clothing

How did all these types meet their antitype in Christ's ministry? The washing and clothing of the Great High Priest is His baptism. **"And it came to pass in those days, that Jesus came from Nazareth of Galilee, and was baptized of John in Jordan"** (Mark 1:9). When Christ presented himself for baptism, John could not understand why the only sinless One upon the earth should ask for an ordinance implying guilt, since through the symbol of baptism people acknowledges they are polluted and need to be washed.

He remonstrated with Christ, acknowledged His superiority, and refused to administer the ordinance, saying, **"I have need to be baptized of thee, and comest thou to me?"** With firm and gentle authority, Jesus waives the refusal of John and his plea of unworthiness, saying, **"Suffer it to be so now; for thus it becometh us to fulfill all righteousness"** (Matt. 3:14, 15).

The fine linen of the priest is the righteousness of Christ, His own unblemished character, woven in the loom of heaven. We are told Christ was made perfect by what he suffered (see Heb. 2:9, 10).

The Anointing of the Priest

What about the anointing of the tabernacle and priest? With what was Jesus anointed? The Bible says, **"How God anointed Jesus of Nazareth with the Holy Ghost and with power: who went about doing good, and healing all that were oppressed of the devil; for God was with him"** (Acts 10:38). When was Jesus anointed? **"And Jesus, when he was baptized, went up straightway out of the water: and, lo, the heavens were opened unto him, and he saw the Spirit of God descending like a dove, and lighting upon him"** (Matt. 3:16).

The word "messiah" means "anointed one." Christ was baptized by John and received the anointing of the Spirit. The Apostle Peter testifies that God anointed Jesus with the Holy Spirit and power. The Savior Himself declared, **"The Spirit of the Lord *is* upon me, because he hath anointed me to preach the gospel to the poor"** (Luke 4:18).

The Killing of the Ram

The killing of the ram typifies the death of Christ on the cross, and the touching of the blood upon Aaron and his sons' ears, thumbs, and toes typifies that by the shedding of the blood Christ, the ear of mercy is now open to the cries of repentant sinners, His feet are willing to come to our aid whenever we seek Him, and His redeeming hands are also stretched out to save.

What does the seething of the consecrating ram's flesh in the Holy Place typify? It typifies the humanity of Christ, wounded and crushed to death before the presence of the Father, now borne into the court of God in the heavenly sanctuary. The priests are commanded to eat the flesh at the door of the tabernacle of the congregation. Here we have a dead ram whose flesh is boiled and a living priest who eats the boiled flesh. One is a dead creature, the other is a living being. What does this typify? It typifies the humanity and divinity of Christ. By eating the flesh, He clothes His divinity with humanity that He might carry all the infirmities and bear all the temptations of our race before the presence of His Father.

What is the function of a door? First of all, a door is a hinged, sliding, or revolving barrier at the entrance to a building. There are three entrances into the earthly tabernacle built by Moses: the first into the courtyard, the second into the Holy Place, and the third into the Most Holy Place. In all cases, they were hanging veils. What does the eating of the flesh at the door of the tabernacle of the congregation typify? The Bible says, **"By a new and living way, which he hath consecrated for us, through the veil, that is to say, his flesh"** (Heb. 10:20).

This symbol typified that by Christ's loving sacrifice, a new way to God's throne has been opened to all who accept Him. Through Jesus, the hidden glory of God's heavenly sanctuary now stands revealed. In taking our nature, the Savior has now bound Himself to humanity by a tie that is never to be broken. In Christ, the family of earth and the family of heaven are now united together. Heaven is enshrined in humanity, and humanity is enfolded in the bosom of infinite love, and through His blessed and precious veil, we now walk through and come before the mercy seat into the presence of God.

Furthermore, the angel said to Daniel that the messiah will **"anoint the most Holy"** (Heb. 9:24). Therefore, in line with type, Christ was to anoint the sanctuary. Did Christ go into the presence of the Lord after the cross? Yes. He was before the Lord as a sacrificial lamb on the cross of Calvary. He was closer as a priest standing before the veil in the Holy

Place. Finally, during the time represented by the Day of Atonement, He stands even closer as the High Priest in front of the ark.

Within the Veil

Does Paul indicate that Christ entered directly into the Most Holy Place at His ascension? **"Which *hope* we have as an anchor of the soul, both sure and stedfast, and which entereth into that within the veil; Whither the forerunner is for us entered,** *even* **Jesus, made an high priest for ever after the order of Melchisedec"** (Heb. 6:19, 20).

We must understand the veil of this chapter within its own context. These and a few earlier verses deal with dispensing the blessings of the Abrahamic covenant to him and his children. This context does not deal with the sanctuary or its apartments, furniture, services, etc., per se. It introduces the veil simply to indicate where Jesus is ministering, where the hope of the covenant people is centered, and from whence the covenant blessings are dispensed. Therefore, it would seem that the word "veil" is used metaphorically to point to the sanctuary as a whole. Unlike Hebrews 9:3, Hebrews 6 makes no attempt to identify which veil it references.

In the original Greek, the term "within the veil" reads *eis to esoteron tou katapetasmatos*. This expression very closely resembles the LXX's (Septuagint—Greek version of the OT) translation of Leviticus 16:2: *eis to hagion esoteron tou katapetasmatos* ["into the holy place within the veil" (RSV)]. The phrase in Leviticus 16:2 differs from that of Hebrews 6:19 only by the addition of *hagion* ("the holy place"). However, there are two things that we must note here.

In the Old Testament, two Hebrew words are used for the veils in the sanctuary: *paroketh* and *masak*. With a few exceptions, *paroketh* refers to the inner veil and *masak* to the veils before the holy place and the courtyard. Some scholars consistently convert *paroketh* to *katapetosma* and *masak* to *kalumma*. Therefore, they say when we read *katapetasma* in Hebrew 6:19, we must understand it as signifying the veil before the Most Holy Place.

However, in Moses' writings, out of the six times he made references to the courtyard, *katapetasma* is used five times. That's true for seven out of eleven occurrences regarding the Holy Place and twenty-three out of twenty-five times for the inner veil. The Septuagint uses *katapetasma* to translate thirty-five of the Pentateuch's forty-two references to the veils, making little distinction as to which veil. Thus, to declare that the veil in Hebrews 6:19 is the inner veil because the LXX uses *katapetasma* is erroneous.

The Right Hand of God

"So then after the Lord had spoken unto them, he was received up into heaven, and sat on the right hand of God" (Mark 16:19).

"Which he wrought in Christ, when he raised him from the dead, and set *him* at his own right hand in the heavenly *places*" (Eph. 1:20).

"But he, being full of the Holy Ghost, looked up steadfastly into heaven, and saw the glory of God, and Jesus standing on the right hand of God, And said, Behold, I see the heavens opened, and the Son of man standing on the right hand of God" (Acts 7:55, 56).

"Who, being the brightness of *his* glory, and the express image of his person, and upholding all things by the word of his power, when he had by himself purged our sins, sat down on the right hand of the Majesty on high" (Heb. 1:3).

The term "right hand" is especially worthy of attention. The Greek is *dexios* and the Hebrew equivalent is *yamiyn*. What is the meaning of this term? Here are some clue the Bible gives: "The right hand of the LORD is exalted: the right hand of the LORD doeth valiantly" (Ps. 118:16). "Now know I that the LORD saveth his anointed; he will hear him from his holy heaven with the saving strength of his right hand" (Ps. 20:6). "Mine hand also hath laid the foundation of the earth, and my right hand hath spanned the heavens: *when* I call unto them, they stand up together" (Isa. 48:13).

Through Jesus, the hidden glory of God's heavenly sanctuary now stands revealed. In taking our nature, the Savior has now bound Himself to humanity by a tie that is never to be broken.

The term "right hand" is employed to represent the absolute will of God, His ultimate purpose, goals, strength, and power. The Bible says:

> The LORD of hosts hath sworn, saying, Surely as I have thought, so shall it come to pass; and as I have purposed, *so* shall it stand... This *is* the purpose that is purposed upon the whole earth: and this *is* the hand that is stretched out upon all the nations. For the LORD of hosts hath purposed, and who shall disannul *it*? and his hand *is* stretched out, and who shall turn it back? (Isa. 14:24–27)

Jesus standing or sitting at the right hand of the Father means occupying the highest place of honor in the heart and government of the

Father and carrying out His purpose and bidding. **"Jesus saith unto him, Thou hast said: nevertheless I say unto you, Hereafter shall ye see the Son of man sitting on the right hand of power, and coming in the clouds of heaven"** (Matt. 26:64). In these words, Christ presented the reverse of the scene then taking place at the judgment hall before the chief priests, elders, and all the council. He, the Lord of life and glory, would be seated at God's right hand. He would be the judge of all the earth, and from His decision there could be no appeal. How do these descriptions of a heavenly sanctuary relate to the work of Christ's priestly service? This we shall learn in the next chapter.

Chapter 8

Open And Shut Door

The book of Revelation takes us through the heavenly sanctuary from the start of intercession in the Holy Place to the unveiling of the Most Holy Place and close of intercession. We will currently focus on the start of intercession in the Holy Place.

> After this I looked, and, behold, a door *was* opened in heaven: and the first voice which I heard *was* as it were of a trumpet talking with me; which said, Come up hither, and I will shew thee things which must be hereafter. And immediately I was in the spirit: and, behold, a throne was set in heaven, and *one* sat on the throne. And he that sat was to look upon like a jasper and a sardine stone: and *there was* a rainbow round about the throne, in sight like unto an emerald. And round about the throne *were* four and twenty seats: and upon the seats I saw four and twenty elders sitting,

> **clothed in white raiment; and they had on their heads crowns of gold. And out of the throne preceded lightnings and thundering and voices: and *there were* seven lamps of fire burning before the throne, which are the seven Spirits of God. And before the throne *there was* a sea of glass like unto crystal: and in the midst of the throne, and round about the throne, *were* four beasts full of eyes before and behind.** (Rev. 4:1–6)

In approximately AD 96, during his exile to the island of Patmos, the Apostle John received instructions to record a special revelation from Jesus. Please notice what John saw. He said that while he was looking into heaven, a door was opened and through it he heard a voice which talked with him and told him to come up so that he could take a view of what is going to happen hereafter.

What did John say he saw? While he was watching, a throne was set and One came and sat on the throne. The Being who came and sat on the throne was said to have the appearance of a jasper and sardius stone. Around the throne was a rainbow-like emerald. Before the throne was something like a sea of glass, or crystal, and there were four living creatures in the midst of and around the throne. Around this throne, there were also other thrones, and upon these thrones were twenty-four elders who were clothed in white raiment and had golden crowns on their heads. What could all these symbols represent?

First of all, in a legal document, "hereafter" could mean "from now on; or at the present," thus implying that some of the things John was shown will take place within the ambit of the first century, his very own days. The message is intentional, purposeful, and decisive.

Before we can move forward through the description of this throne scene, we need to note that this is not the first time these images were recorded. First of all, the Prophet Ezekiel also records a similar throne scene, although in his description, there were no twenty-four elders around, and the four, living creature were beneath the throne.

> **And the likeness of the firmament upon the heads of the living creature *was* as the colour of the terrible crystal, stretched forth over their heads above. And under the firmament *were* their wings straight, the one toward the other: every one had two, which covered on this side, and every one had two, which covered on that side, their bodies.... And above the firmament that *was* over their heads *was* the likeness of a throne, as the appearance of a sapphire**

> stone: and upon the likeness of the throne *was* the likeness as the appearance of a man above upon it.... As the appearance of the bow that is in the cloud in the day of rain, so *was* the appearance of the brightness round about. This *was* the appearance of the likeness of the glory of the LORD. And when I saw *it*, I fell upon my face, and I heard a voice of one that spake." (Ezek. 1:22–28)

As you can see, the throne is above the heads of the four, living creatures. Nevertheless, the scene pictured by John the revelator is a little different from that of Ezekiel in that the four living creatures were not beneath the throne this time, but right in the midst of and around the throne, showing that the throne stepped down. You will better understand the scene when you take the phrase "a throne was set in heaven" into consideration. What does it mean?

A Throne Was Set in Heaven

Before we interpret the whole phrase, let us first get a general understanding of the word "set." In consulting with *The Cassel Concise Dictionary* (1998, p. 1348), "set" is defined as "established," which coincides with *The Oxford Universal Dictionary* (1955, p. 634). Taking this into consideration, we can reckon that a throne will be set up and placed where it was not placed before in heaven. There is no doubt this is taking place in the first apartment of the heavenly sanctuary.

Where do we find the seven lamps of fire in the Hebrew sanctuary? They were in the Holy Place. In Revelation 4, the throne is where the seven branch candlesticks are. The phrase about the throne being "set" shows a rearrangement. In Chapter 7 of this book, we learned that the throne of God is high above the mercy seat, while every other thing in the sanctuary is below. A careful reader will notice the conspicuous absence of God's Son, Jesus.

The Lamb with Seven Eyes

> And I saw in the right hand of him that sat on the throne a book written within and on the backside, sealed with seven seals. And I saw a strong angel proclaiming with a loud voice, Who is worthy to open the book, and to loose the seals thereof? And no man in heaven, nor in earth, neither under the earth, was able to open the book, neither to look thereon. And I wept much, because no man was found worthy to open and to read the book, neither to look thereon. And one of the elders saith unto me, Weep not: behold,

the Lion of the tribe of Juda, the Root of David, hath prevailed to open the book, and to loose the seven seals thereof. And I beheld, and, lo, in the midst of the throne and of the four beasts, and in the midst of the elders, stood a Lamb as it had been slain, having seven horns and seven eyes, which are the seven Spirits of God sent forth into all the earth.** (Rev. 5:1–6)

There are two important points that I want you to see here. The first is that this Lamb is seen with **"seven eyes, which are the seven Spirits of God sent forth into all the earth."** Here we are dealing with the omnipresence of the Son of God by the Holy Spirit. The fact that this Spirit is sent throughout the whole earth is how we know that His omnipresence is being declared. The second point is that this Lamb is seen **"as it had been slain."** In other words, John sees blood. What next? **"And he came and took the book out of the right hand of him that sat upon the throne"** (v. 7).

Please note the phrase **"when He had taken the book"** (v. 8). Who took the book? Jesus did. The Bible says the Lamb came and took the book from the hand of Him who sat on the throne.

The Seven Horns of the Lamb

Describing the Lamb of God, the Bible says He has seven horns. And what does this typify? Well, for what it's worth, it is interesting to note that Jesus had seven wounded spots: head, two hands, two feet, side, and back. In any event, the number seven is the number for perfection. Christ was our perfect sacrifice who was slain from the foundation of the world. It is also interesting to note that there were seven applications/locations of blood in the ancient, Jewish ritual:

1. The first application of blood was the rectification of the covenant: **"And he took the book of the covenant, and read in the audience of the people: and they said, All that the LORD hath said will we do, and be obedient. And Moses took the blood, and sprinkled** *it* **on the people, and said, Behold the blood of the covenant, which the LORD hath made with you concerning all these words"** (Exod. 24:7, 8).

2. Second, there was the remission of sin through the application of blood on the horns of the altar of sacrifice: **"And thou shalt kill the bullock before the LORD,** *by* **the door of the tabernacle of the congregation. And thou shalt take of the blood of the bullock, and put** *it* **upon the horns of the altar with thy finger** (Exod. 29:11, 12).

3. The third place was at the laver, a place of washing, where the blood mingled with the water as the priests washed their hands and feet: **"Thou shalt also make a laver *of* brass, and his foot *also of* brass, to wash *withal*: and thou shalt put it between the tabernacle of the congregation and the altar, and thou shalt put water therein" (Exod. 30:18).

4. The fourth place was upon the horns of the altar of incense, where the blood and incense interacted: "And he shall go out unto the altar that *is* before the LORD, and make an atonement for it; and shall take of the blood of the bullock, and of the blood of the goat, and put *it* upon the horns of the altar round about" (Lev. 16:18).

5. The fifth place was before the veil: "And the priest shall dip his finger in the blood, and sprinkle of the blood seven times before the LORD, before the veil of the sanctuary" (Lev. 4:6)

6. The sixth place was upon the mercy seat: "And he shall take of the blood of the bullock, and sprinkle *it* with his finger upon the mercy seat eastward; and before the mercy seat shall he sprinkle of the blood with his finger seven times" (Lev. 16:14).

7. The last place was at the base of the altar of sacrifice: "And thou shalt take of the blood of the bullock…and pour all the blood beside the bottom of the altar" (Exod. 29:12).

Just as the altar lifted up the sacrifice, so Jesus had to be lifted up to draw all people to Himself. Christ was made a curse in our stead. We saw that the altar had four horns. It is interesting to note that God wants to offer us the power of forgiveness, self-denial, overcoming, and obedience. God requires the entire surrender of the heart before justification can take place, and in order for people to retain justification, there must be continual obedience through active, living faith that works by love and purifies the soul. Justification starts at the altar. The Holy and the Most Holy Places help us stay dedicated through the power of the horns.

The Twenty-Four Elders

Please note that each of the twenty-four elders has a golden censer full of incense, and this incense is said to be prayers of the saints. Who are these twenty-four elders? Who are seated on the thrones round about God's throne? They have crowns on their heads. They are robed in white garments of light. In fact, look at what happens to the twenty-four elders once the slain Lamb was seen. "And when he had taken the book, the four beasts and four *and* twenty elders fell down before the Lamb, having every one of them harps, and golden vials full of odours, which are the prayers of saints" (Rev. 5:8).

There is a clear transition that occurs with these elders. Whereas previously they were seen with crowns and in white robes, now they are seen with harps and golden bowls of incense. If you go back to the OT, you will see that King David, when establishing the order for the earthly temple, actually established twenty-four orders of musicians to serve in the temple and twenty-four orders of priests to burn incense (see 1 Chron. 24:1–19; 25:1–31). What specific action was one of the elders found doing when John was weeping?

"And I wept much, because no man was found worthy to open and to read the book, neither to look thereon. And one of the elders saith unto me, Weep not: behold, the Lion of the tribe of Juda, the Root of David, hath prevailed to open the book, and to loose the seven seals thereof" (Rev. 5:4, 5). The vision, as presented to John, made its impression upon his mind. The destiny of every nation was contained in that book.

> John was distressed at the utter inability of any human being or angelic intelligence to read the words, or even to look thereon. His soul was wrought up to such a point of agony and suspense that one of the strong angels had compassion on him, and laying his hand on him assuringly, said, "Weep not: behold, the Lion of the tribe of Juda, the Root of David, hath prevailed to open the book, and to loose the seven seals thereof" [verse 5]. (White, *Manuscript Release*, vol. 12, pp. 296–7)

Therefore, from the above inspired counsel, we can see that the twenty-four elders are a powerful, angelic host around the throne of God, with a special task of leading the heavenly choir and offering incense on the golden altar of incense before the throne of God. They were to serve in a priestly capacity in the heavenly sanctuary. As it was in the earthly, so it is in the heavenly.

The Lamb coming to receive the book from Him who sat on the throne points to the coming of Christ to the Holy Place of the heavenly sanctuary. This is the beginning or inauguration of His priestly function. When the Son of God shed His blood and returned to heaven, He reclaimed His glory and began his work of intercession in the heavenly sanctuary.

Now this brings us to our next question: To where does the first open door lead? According to Revelation 4, the open door leads into the sanctuary in heaven, specifically the Holy Place. We see the seven lamps before throne, as well as the golden vials of incense. At which time in history was this door opened? At the ascension of Christ, for we see Him identified as a lamb slain, and by reason of His death he was declared worthy to fulfill the tasks of salvation.

At Christ's ascension to heaven, the door to the Holy Place was opened for humanity. A new and living way is now opened to the fallen race. All sacrificial offerings are terminated in the one great offering of the Son of God. Having now entered by His own blood into the heavenly sanctuary, He began the work of intercession.

As in the earthly sanctuary, there were two distinct apartments in the heavenly sanctuary, so in its antitype each division of the work of Christ has its distinctive place. Thus, when He ascended, having offered Himself here on earth, he went directly through the first veil into the Holy Place of the heavenly sanctuary where He was anointed as High Priest to begin His work as intercessor.

The Shut Door

How is the divine Being who addressed the church at Philadelphia described? What title does the angel gave him? **"And to the angel of the church in Philadelphia write; These things saith he that is holy, he that is true, he that hath the key of David, he that openeth, and no man shutteth; and shutteth, and no man openeth; I know thy works: behold, I have set before thee an open door, and no man can shut it: for thou hast a little strength, and hast kept my word, and hast not denied my name"** (Rev. 3:7, 8).

The living Christ is altogether holy, and His words are eternally true. He Himself addresses John, declaring amazing, end-time truth. Which door is shut? And which door is opened? We see Christ, who holds the keys, shutting a door that no man can open and opening a door which no man can shut, and this happen during the Philadelphia period.

To properly understand this message, we must first look at the Bible reference to the seven churches of Asia Minor. Jesus appeared to John, **"Saying, I am Alpha and Omega, the first and the last: and, What thou seest, write in a book, and send *it* unto the seven churches which are in Asia; unto Ephesus, and unto Smyrna, and unto Pergamos, and unto Thyatira, and unto Sardis, and unto Philadelphia, and unto Laodicea"** (Rev. 1:11).

John's letters to the seven churches were addressed to actual groups of Christian believers in the Roman province of Asia. These churches were in existence in the cities with these names. There were more than seven cities where Christian churches existed, but only seven were chosen to which Jesus sent special messages.

The seven letters to the churches correlate closely with the periods and events of church history. Multiple, post-Reformation scholars recognized the seven churches as spanning the Christian era. For instance, Adam Burwell wrote in 1835, "The seven churches typify the church universal in its seven ages from Pentecost till the day of the Lord" (*Prophetic Faith of Our Fathers*, vol. 4, 313).

The Seven Churches

CHURCH TIME PERIODS (dates are approximate)

1. Ephesus—AD 31–100
2. Smyrna—AD 100–313
3. Pergamos—AD 313–538
4. Thyatira—AD 538–1517
5. Sardis—AD 1517–1798
6. Philadelphia—AD 1798–1845
7. Laodicea—AD 1845–The End

A study of history reveals that these messages are indeed applicable in a special way to seven successive periods that cover the entire history of the Christian church. The seven churches represent the one Christian church going through seven periods of time. In other words, the seven literal churches of Asian Minor are actually symbolic of seven successive stages of church history from the beginning of Christian era to the end of time.

To the Jews, the number seven indicates completeness and is symbolic of the fact that the messages extend to the end of time, while the symbols used reveal the condition of the church at different periods in the history of the world. There are three conclusions that can be reached based on this study:

First, the seven churches, according to most conservative scholars, represent the seven successive stages in the history of the Christian church from the days of the apostles until the end of time.

Second, the church of Ephesus fitly symbolized the character and condition of the church in its first state, during the first century, the apostolic period when its members received the doctrine of Christ in its purity and enjoyed the benefits and blessings of the gifts of the Holy Spirit. This marks and symbolizes the beginning of the history of the seven churches, while Philadelphia, the sixth church comes toward the close of earth's history.

Third, the seventh church is the last church of the Christian era. It's interesting to note that the name "Laodicea" means "judging the people" (Greek *Laodikeus*, from *Laodikeia*—"justice of the people").

The Key of David

Who has the key of David? Jesus does. You'll notice the key was to open something and also shut something, and nobody can reverse these actions. What does the key open? The key of David opens a door. To where does this door lead? Let's first understand what this key of David is all about. In order to understand the mystery about the key of David in Revelation 3, we go back to the OT source. This expression comes from Isaiah. It is a messianic prophecy. **"And the key of the house of David will I lay upon his shoulder; so he shall open, and none shall shut; and he shall shut, and none shall open. And I will fasten him *as* a nail in a sure place; and he shall be for a glorious throne to his father's house"** (Rev. 22:22, 23).

There are some details here that are not found in Revelation 3. We are told that this key would be laid on the Messiah's shoulder. He would also be fastened as a nail in a sure place and become a glorious throne to His Father's house. Here we have the idea of kingship.

Isaiah made another reference to the Messiah's shoulder. **"For unto us a child is born, unto us a son is given: and the government shall be upon his shoulder"** (Rev. 9:6). With both the key of David and government placed on the Messiah's shoulder, this would suggest that the key was given to open the entrance door to the Messiah's government. Talking about the same individual, Isaiah continues: **"Of the increase of *his* government and peace *there shall be* no end, upon the throne of David, and upon his kingdom, to order it, and to establish it with judgment and with justice from henceforth even for ever"** (v. 7).

What does the key help Him do? The key opens the entrance door to His government. As He sat on the throne to rule, we are told that He would order and establish His government with judgment and justice. We are told the Messiah will be sitting on the throne of David forever. It is impressive to see how these details piece together.

Going further, if He is going into the door, what is the purpose? He is going to get His kingdom by performing a work of judgment, a theme found in Revelation 3, which naturally segues to the eternal establishment of His government. The fact is that the book of Revelation mentions two doors. We've carefully identified the first door, which leads to the first apartment of the heavenly sanctuary.

It is interesting to note that Christ's death on the cross corresponded to the moment when, on the Day of Atonement, the high priest killed the Lord's goat in the outer court. The death of the goat is necessary, for without its blood, there could be no atonement. However, the death itself was not the complete atonement, though it was the necessary first step. Therefore, the cross is the first (not only) phase of Christ's work as the suffering sacrifice.

The second phase began immediately after His ascension. He began His work as our High Priest, in harmony with the typical service. He must plead His blood before the Father, for without the ministration of His blood, His death is useless. It is the blood that counts. The Bible says, **"And to Jesus the mediator of the new covenant, and to the blood of sprinkling, that speaketh better things than *that of* Abel"** (Heb. 12:24). It is the blood of Jesus sprinkled before the Father that atones for our sins. Christ began pleading before the Father the cases of repenting, believing sinners, presenting to Him the offering of His own blood on their behalf. The first open door leads to the Holy Place, where Christ accomplishes the second phase of His work.

While the First Door Is Still Open

Ever since His ascension, what has been the main work of our High Priest in the first apartment of the heavenly sanctuary? **"Neither by the blood of goats and calves, but by his own blood had he entered in once into the holy place, having obtained eternal redemption *for us*"** (Heb. 9:12). **"But this *man*, because he continueth ever, hath an unchangeable priesthood. Wherefore he is able also to save them to the uttermost that come unto God by him, seeing he ever liveth to make intercession for them. For such an high priest became us, *who is* holy, harmless, undefiled, separate from sinners, and made higher than the heavens"** (Heb. 7:24–26).

> **Christ Jesus is represented as continually standing at the altar, momentarily offering up the sacrifice for the sins of the world. He is a minister of the true tabernacle which the Lord pitched and not man.... Jesus is officiating in the presence of God, offering up His shed blood, as it had been a lamb slain. (White, Selected Messages, book 1, pp. 343–4)**

How effective are the merits of Christ's blood while the probationary door of the first apartment is open? **"And from Jesus Christ, *who is* the faithful witness, *and* the first begotten of the dead, and the prince of the kings of the earth. Unto him that loved us, and washed us from our sins in his own blood"** (Rev. 1:5). **"How much more shall the blood of Christ, who through the eternal Spirit offered himself without spot to God, purge**

your conscience from dead works to serve the living God" (Heb. 9:14)? **"If we confess our sins, he is faithful and just to forgive us *our* sins, and to cleanse us from all unrighteousness"** (1 John 1:9).

Jesus presents the oblation offered for every offense and shortcoming of the sinner. The relations between God and each soul are as distinct and full as though there were not another soul upon the earth to share His watch care, nor for whom He gave His Beloved Son.

Christ, our Mediator, and the Holy Spirit are constantly interceding on humanity's behalf, but the Spirit pleads not for us as does Christ, who presents His blood, shed from the foundation of the world. The Spirit works upon our hearts, drawing out prayers, penitence, praise, and thanksgiving to Christ. The gratitude which flows from our lips is the result of the Spirit striking the chords of the soul in holy memories, awakening the music of the heart and drawing it to Christ. Now let's return back to our study of the second door, which was opened during the Philadelphia church age. The declaration is in Revelation 11.

The Second Door

"And the temple of God was opened in heaven, and there was seen in his temple the ark of his testament: and there were lightnings, and voices, and thunderings, and an earthquake, and great hail" (Rev. 11:19). **"And after that I looked, and, behold, the temple of the tabernacle of the testimony in heaven was opened"** (Rev. 15:5).

Please note that the Bible texts we read say the temple in heaven was open. *Naos* is the Greek word that was used, which points specifically to the inner shrine of the temple—the Most Holy Place. This is where the ark of the covenant is located. We discovered that the reason the ark in the earthly sanctuary was called the "ark of the testimony" was because of its contents—the Ten Commandments. **"And he took and put the testimony into the ark, and set the staves on the ark, and put the mercy seat above upon the ark"** (Exod. 40:20).

If the Most Holy Place of the heavenly sanctuary was being opened, it means it must have been closed. With what was it opened? The key of David. As soon as the door of the inner shrine was opened, what was seen? The ark of the covenant. The first door was opened when Jesus ascended into heaven, during the first century of the Christian era (Ephesus), while the second door was open at the pivot of the two, final church eras (Philadelphia and Laodicea). Let's look at this subject from another perspective.

The Ancient of Days

Daniel adequately portrays the glory and solemnity of the Most Holy Place of the heavenly court. He gives us an accurate account of the opening day:

> I beheld till the thrones were cast down, and the Ancient of days did sit, whose garment *was* white as snow, and the hair of his head like the pure wool: his throne *was like* the fiery flame, *and* his wheels as burning fire. A fiery stream issued and came forth from before him: thousand thousands ministered unto him, and ten thousand times ten thousand stood before him: the judgment was set, and the books were opened. (Dan. 7:9, 10)

This is a very interesting expression. Daniel said he beheld until the thrones were cast down. The term "cast down" means "to bring down from a higher position" or "re-positioning, placed, or re-arrangement." These phrases suggest a movement of the throne of God.

The reference to the throne is plural, indicating that more than one throne was set. Since God's throne is originally set above the mercy seat, we are told in His Word that the throne of the mercy seat is situated in between the covering cherubim, above the ark of covenant in the Most Holy Place of the heavenly sanctuary. It is also evident that besides this throne are other, lesser thrones placed in position as well.

Antitype of the Sanctuary Record

"The judgment was set, and the books were open." This is Daniel's description of the heavenly courtroom—the supreme court of the universe in session. Before the Sovereign of the whole universe stood billions of angels ready to minister before Him. Which books are Daniel referencing? "Behold, *it is* written before me...Your iniquities, and the iniquities of your fathers together, saith the LORD" (Isa. 65:6, 7). "And the LORD said unto Moses, Whosoever hath sinned against me, him will I blot out of my book" (Exod. 32:33).

There is a record of the sins of humanity in heaven. Besides this record, we also have the book of remembrance containing the good deeds of humanity. "Then they that feared the LORD spake often one to another: and the LORD hearkened, and heard *it*, and a book of remembrance was written before him for them that feared the LORD, and that thought upon his name" (Mal. 3:16). "Remember me, O my God, concerning this, and wipe not out my good deeds that I have done for the house of my God, and for the offices thereof" (Neh. 13:14).

Besides these books of records, God also has a book containing our pain and sorrows. There, every temptation resisted, every sin confessed, every evil overcome, every word of kindness, prayer, and testimony is faithfully chronicled, and every act of sacrifice, every suffering and sorrow endured for Christ's sake, is recorded. Says the psalmist, "Thou tellest my wanderings: put thou my tears into thy bottle: *are they* not in thy book" (Ps. 56:8)? God's Word also says, "He that overcometh, the same shall be clothed in white raiment; and I will not blot out his name out of the book of life, but I will confess his name before my Father, and before his angels" (Rev. 3:5).

Dear Christian friends, how will you stand in the judgment? What will the record show? Will you be found faithful? Have you repented of every sin? When your name is called, what will be the result? Notice what Daniel saw next:

> I saw in the night visions, and, behold, *one* like the Son of man came with the clouds of heaven, and came to the Ancient of days, and they brought him near before him. And there was given him dominion, and glory, and a kingdom, that all people, nations, and languages, should serve him: his dominion *is* an everlasting dominion, which shall not pass away, and his kingdom *that* which shall not be destroyed. (Dan. 7:13, 14)

Jesus is here introduced as One who is connected to humanity. He came to the Ancient of days, but this coming cannot represent His return to the earth. It represents His movement as our High Priest into the Most Holy Place.

The Bible says, "We have this as a sure and steadfast anchor of the soul, a hope that enters into the inner place behind the curtain, where Jesus has gone as a forerunner on our behalf, having become a high priest forever after the order of Melchizedek" (Heb. 6:19, 20, ESV). With this understanding, we affirmed that the first door was

> *The relations between God and each soul are as distinct and full as though there were not another soul upon the earth to share His watch care, nor for whom He gave His Beloved Son.*

opened when Jesus ascended into heaven, during the first century of the Christian era, while the second door was opened at the approach of the closing period of the church era, under the sixth church, Philadelphia. This opening phased into the last church period, Laodicea. At what particular date in history was this second door that leads to the Most Holy Place opened?

CHAPTER 9

The Vision Of The Evening And Morning

This chapter takes us through an important prophetic message—the vision of the evening and morning. The angel said to Daniel, **"And he said unto me, Unto two thousand and three hundred days [Hebrew** *ereb boqer*— **"evening morning"]; then shall the sanctuary be cleansed"** (8:14). Daniel 8 is divided into two parts. The first fourteen verses contain symbols and prophecies. The remainder contains interpretations. Gabriel interpreted all the symbols in this vision to the prophet Daniel, except for the 2,300 days.

This symbolic prophecy has intrigued believers ever since it was first penned by the Prophet Daniel. To understand its message and how it concerns believers living in these last days, we will, in this chapter, endeavor to identify the following:

1. When was this prophecy given?
2. What does the ram with two horns symbolize?
3. What does the rough he goat symbolize?
4. In Bible prophecy, what do horns symbolize? Who/what is the great horn that was broken? Who/what are the four horns that replace it?
5. Who/what is the little horn?
6. Where is the sanctuary that is polluted?
7. Who constitutes the heavenly host that the little horn cast down to the earth?
8. Who is the Prince of princes?
9. What is the daily sacrifice?
10. What is the meaning of the evening and morning?
11. How long is 2,300 days?
12. When do the 2,300 days begin?
13. How does this prophecy concern us?

When Was This Prophecy Given?

"In the third year of the reign of king Belshazzar a vision appeared unto me, *even unto* me Daniel, after that which appeared unto me at the first" (Dan. 8:1). It was given in the third year of King Belshazzar, which was about 553 BC.

What Does the Ram with Two Horns Symbolize?

"The ram which thou sawest having *two* horns *are* the kings of Media and Persia" (Dan. 8:1).

What Does the Rough He Goat Symbolize?

"And the rough goat *is* the king of Grecia" (v. 21). In other words, these two beasts represented the ancient empires that came after the Babylonian Empire, which ended when King Belshazzar died.

What do horns symbolize? Who/what is the great horn? four horns?

In Bible prophecy, a horn is a symbol of a king(dom). "And the ten horns which thou sawest are ten kings" (Rev. 17:12). Gabriel told Daniel the first horn was the first king of Greece. The first earthly king of Greece was Alexander the Great. His military might enabled him to overthrow the Medo-Persian Empire, symbolized in this prophecy by the ram.

At the time of Alexander's death, his dominion was assumed by his four generals: Cassander—Macedonia; Seleucus—Syria; Lysimachus—Asia Minor; Ptolemy—Egypt.

Who/What is the Little Horn?

Gabriel told Daniel that *"out of one of them came forth a little horn, which waxed exceeding great, toward the south, and toward the east, and toward the pleasant land"* (Dan. 8:9). We should begin by noting that the focus of Daniel 8 is the little horn, just like the little horn of Daniel 7. Six verses are devoted to the description of the ram and goat.

The origins of the little horn give little indication of the power and prominence to which this king eventually attains.

After the one large horn of the goat is broken off (apparently the death of Alexander the Great), four inferior horns arise. The little horn emerges from one of these four horns. While rather small at first, it grows to be exceedingly great. *"And it waxed great, even to the host of heaven; and it cast down some of the host and of the stars to the ground, and stamped upon them"* (v. 10).

The conflict between the little horn and God becomes almost bigger than life at this point. In the previous verse, the little horn achieves things which are more than human. He grows up to the host of heaven, causing some of the stars to fall to the earth, where he tramples them. Like the ram and goat before him, he magnified himself. *"Yea, he magnified himself even to the prince of the host, and by him the daily sacrifice was taken away, and the place of his sanctuary was cast down"* (v. 11).

While the others magnified themselves above men, this horn magnifies himself to be equal with the Prince of the host. He removes the regular sacrifice from Him and throws down the place of His sanctuary. This king thinks himself equal with God, going as far as directly opposing God. The little horn seems to change before our eyes, from a mortal man to an incarnation of Satan himself. The focus seems to shift from the Israelites, Israel, Jerusalem, and the temple to the host of heaven. This prophecy suggests that much more exists here than meets the eye. It is little wonder that Bible students differ greatly regarding the meaning of these verses.

The evidence is plain that the little horn of Daniel 7 is the same as the one in Daniel 8. For instance, the following was written about the little horn in the former:

> I considered the horns, and, behold, there came up among them another little horn, before whom there were three of the first horns plucked up by the roots: and, behold, in this horn *were* eyes like the eyes of man, and a mouth speaking great things.... And he shall speak *great* words against the most High, and shall wear out the saints of the most High, and think to change times and laws: and they shall be given into his hand until a time and times and the dividing of time. (Dan. 7:8, 25)

Although some commentators have expressed the view that the little horn power of Daniel 8 symbolizes Antiochus Epiphanies, a careful examination of this prophecy and evidence proves beyond a reasonable doubt that the Seleucid king does not in any way fulfill the criteria.

For example, the four horns of the goat were kingdoms, so it is expected the little horn is a kingdom too. However, Antiochus was only one king of the four kingdoms, specifically the Seleucid Empire. Therefore, he could not be another complete horn. Furthermore, the abomination of desolation described by Daniel was yet future, even in Jesus' day, and had nothing to do whatsoever with the Antiochus (centuries before Christ). Christ referred to the event as being future, not past.

Where Is the Sanctuary That Is Polluted?

There are three places where the word "sanctuary" was mentioned in Daniel 8 (vs. 11, 13, and 14). The Hebrew word used for "sanctuary" in verse 11 is *miqdash*, while the word used in verses 13 and 14 is *qodesh*. Why are there two different words employed in the description of the sanctuary in Daniel 8?

As we attempt to answer this, I'd like us to first look at the full meaning of the word *miqdash*. It refers to a consecrated thing, as well as a hallowed part of the sanctuary. *Miqdash* is a common term in the OT for the sanctuary. On the other hand, the word *qodesh* not only refers to the sanctuary as a whole, but focuses on the Holy and Most Holy Places. *Qodesh* is the word used throughout Leviticus 16.

Now this brings us to another important question: Which sanctuary was cast down? Gabriel said in verse 11, **"the place of his** [*the little horn*] **sanctuary was cast down."**

The word "place" is *mekon* in Hebrew and used to designate "site." "Site" means "a place where something is located or has occurred" (Concise Oxford English Dictionary, Eleventh Edition).

It could mean "abode." It is used to designate a base. It points to the

The Vision Of The Evening And Morning | 103

seat of the little horn. One might ask the question, "How do you know that it is the place of Christ's sanctuary and not a pagan sanctuary that is cast down?" The Bible says, **"Who opposeth and exalteth himself above all that is called God, or that is worshipped; so that he as God sitteth in the temple of God, showing himself that he is God"** (2 Thess. 2:4). This confirmed it. How did the little horn cast down the place of His sanctuary? **"And an host was given [him] against the daily [sacrifice] by reason of transgression, and it cast down the truth to the ground; and it practiced, and prospered"** (Dan. 8:12).

It was by transgression—casting down the truth to the ground—that His place of sanctuary was cast down. When Daniel 8:11 is compared with Daniel 11:31, it appears to make more sense. Gabriel says, **"And arms shall stand on his part, and they shall pollute the sanctuary of strength, and shall take away the daily *sacrifice*, and they shall place the abomination that maketh desolate."**

What is this sanctuary of strength? The Bible says, **"Now therefore arise, O LORD God, into thy resting place, thou, and the ark of thy strength: let thy priests, O LORD God, be clothed with salvation, and let thy saints rejoice in goodness"** (2 Chron. 6:41). **"Arise, O LORD, into thy rest; thou, and the ark of thy strength"** (Ps. 132:8). The sanctuary of strength denotes the most hallowed part of the sanctuary that contains the ark of God's strength. What makes it the ark God's strength? ***"There was nothing in the ark save the two tables of stone, which Moses put there at Horeb, when the LORD made* a covenant *with the children of Israel, when they came out of the land of Egypt"*** (1 King 8:9).

It's the law of God in the ark that makes the ark God's strength. The law is the strength of sin. The Bible says **"The sting of death [is] sin; and the strength of sin *is* the law"** (1 Cor. 15:56). The Law is the focus here. Therefore, the truth that was cast down was the law of God. By the attack on the law, the sanctuary was polluted. The Bible says, **"Her prophets *are* light [and] treacherous persons: her priests have polluted the sanctuary, they have done violence to the law"** (Zeph. 3:4).

In Daniel 8:13, a question was asked about how long the sanctuary should be tread down, and the answer follows in verse 14.

Who Is this Heavenly Host?

The word "host" comes from the Hebrew *tsaba' tseba'ah*, which alludes to a mass of people, especially organized for war. The word is used five times in Daniel 8:10–13. The heavenly hosts, as described in the condition of the night of Jesus' birth, are angels. **"And suddenly there was with the angel a multitude of the *heavenly host* praising God, and saying, Glory to God in the highest, and on earth peace, good will toward men"** (Luke 2:13, 14, emphasis mine).

What special task has God entrusted to them? From the beautiful words of inspiration, we read, **"Who maketh his angels spirits;"** also, **"Are they not all ministering spirits, sent forth to minister for them who shall be heirs of salvation"** (Ps. 104:4; Heb. 1:14)? The heavenly hosts are entrusted with the task of ministering to the saints. Jesus says, **"Take heed that ye despise not one of these little ones; for I say unto you, That in heaven their angels do always behold the face of my Father which is in heaven"** (Matt. 18:10).

There is no doubt that God's angels guard and protect each believer. They also convey and flash heavenly truth to the minds of believers. Daniel, in a holy vision, saw the little horn casting down the heavenly host to the ground. The question is, "In what way is the heavenly host cast down to the ground? **"And his power shall be mighty, but not by his own power: and he shall destroy wonderfully, and shall prosper, and practice, and shall destroy the mighty and the holy people"** (Dan. 8:24).

How strikingly this prophecy was fulfilled in the great persecution of the Dark Ages, when millions of saints where murdered in cold blood for their faith. The man of sin and son of perdition (see 2 Thess. 2:3) seemed to take over the church. The Apostle Paul describes this time in the following words: **"Who opposeth and exalteth himself above all that is called God, or that is worshipped; so that he as God sitteth in the temple of God, shewing himself that he is God"** (v. 4).

Daniel 8:12 puts the success of the little horn, as described in the two previous verses, in perspective. One may gain the impression that the horn takes on God and wins. The reality is that the host of heaven was displaced by the horn, not because of the horn's greatness, but on account of the transgression of God's people. Truth is cast to the ground. **"And judgment is turned away backward, and justice standeth afar off: for truth is fallen in the street, and equity cannot enter. Yea, truth faileth; and he *that* departeth from evil maketh himself a prey"** (Isa. 59:14, 15). Everything the little horn attempts seems to succeed, even his rebellion against God, His people, and holy place.

Who is the Prince of Princes?

The Hebrew word *sar*, translated "prince," is related to a verb meaning "to exercise dominion." A prince is one who will one day be king, but does not currently hold that position. In addition to referring to the son of a king or person of royal rank, the word applies to a head or chief. The term "Prince of princes" in Daniel 8:25 comes from the Hebrew *sar sarim* and is axiomatic of one who is the greatest prince of all. To say that God (the Son) is Prince of princes is to say that He rules all other rulers. In the same way, He is King of kings and Lord of lords. The NT confirms that Jesus is the One to whom this title applies with multiple references (see Acts 3:15; 5:31; Rev. 1:5).

Daniel further reveals the wicked activities of the little horn, which seem more audacious considering what we concluded above. "**And through his policy also he shall cause craft to prosper in his hand; and he shall magnify *himself* in his heart, and by peace shall destroy many: he shall also stand up against the Prince of princes; but he shall be broken without hand**" (Dan. 8:25).

What is the Daily Sacrifice?

The "daily" (from the Hebrew *tamiyd*) is mentioned five times in the Bible, all of which are in Daniel:

> **Yea, he magnified *himself* even to the prince of the host, and by him the daily *sacrifice* was taken away, and the place of his sanctuary was cast down. And an host was given *him* against the daily *sacrifice* by reason of transgression, and it cast down the truth to the ground; and it practised, and prospered. Then I heard one saint speaking, and another saint said unto that certain *saint* which spake, How long *shall be* the vision *concerning* the daily *sacrifice*, and the transgression of desolation, to give both the sanctuary and the host to be trodden under foot? (Dan. 8:11–13)**

> **And arms shall stand on his part, and they shall pollute the sanctuary of strength, and shall take away the daily *sacrifice*, and they shall place the abomination that maketh desolate. (Dan. 11:31)**

> **And from the time *that* the daily *sacrifice* shall be taken away, and the abomination that maketh desolate set up, *there shall be* a thousand two hundred and ninety days. (Dan. 12:11)**

A study of this word reveals that it was used in connection with many activities the priests performed in their daily work in the sanctuary. It is usually used as an adjective before various, continuous activities, or as an adverb following activities. Thus, we see that the phrase "take away

106 | *The Final Atonement*

the daily" is filled with sanctuary language. The daily was operated in the earthly sanctuary. In the days of antiquity, under the old covenant, the priest would offer a sacrifice in the morning *and* evening, confessing the sins of Israel and reconciling them with their Maker.

However, under the new covenant relationship, in which believers are recognized as priests, the Bible says, **"Let my prayer be set forth before thee** *as* **incense;** *and* **the lifting up of my hands** *as* **the evening sacrifice"** (Ps. 141:2). **"And another angel came and stood at the altar, having a golden censer; and there was given unto him much incense, that he should offer** *it* **with the prayers of all saints upon the golden altar which was before the throne. And the smoke of the incense,** *which came* **with the prayers of the saints, ascended up before God out of the angel's hand"** (Rev. 8:3, 4).

The sacrifice we offer to God is our prayers and worship. Taking away the daily sacrifice, on a personal level, means taking away our right and freedom to worship God in purity and holiness.

What is the Meaning of the Evening and Morning?

The fact that the phrase "evening and morning" was used in Daniel 8:14 instead of the word "day" perhaps stifled Daniel's understanding, causing a wonderment which, for a time, made him feel sick. The phrase calls our minds to Genesis 1, where this expression is repeatedly used to describe twenty-four-hour days. **"And God called the light Day, and the darkness he called Night. And the evening and the morning were the first day"** (v. 5). The phrase does not refer to the Hebrew sacrifices. Why not? Because whenever such reference is made in connection with the sacrificial offering, the phrase is always "morning and evening"; the morning offering came first, then the evening followed.

> **Behold, I build an house to the name of the LORD my God, to dedicate** *it* **to him,** *and* **to burn before him sweet incense, and for the continual showbread, and for the burnt offerings** *morning and evening***, on the sabbaths, and on the new moons, and on the solemn feasts of the LORD our God. This** *is an ordinance* **for ever to Israel.** (2 Chron. 2:4, third emphasis mine)

> **And king Ahaz commanded Urijah the priest, saying, Upon the great altar burn the morning burnt offering, and the evening meat offering, and the king's burnt sacrifice, and his meat offering, with the burnt offering of all the people of the land, and their meat offering, and their drink offerings; and sprinkle upon it all**

> **the blood of the burnt offering, and all the blood of the sacrifice: and the brazen altar shall be for me to inquire** *by*. (2 Kings 16:15)

> **And they burn unto the LORD every morning and every evening burnt sacrifices and sweet incense: the shewbread also** *set they in order* **upon the pure table; and the candlestick of gold with the lamps thereof, to burn every evening: for we keep the charge of the LORD our God; but ye have forsaken him.** (2 Chron. 13:11)

You can see that "morning and evening" was used in reference to the burnt offering. However, in Daniel 8:14, the evening comes first, before the morning, because it's referring to twenty-four-hour days. On God's calendar, each day begins at evening. The use of the phrase "morning and evening sacrifice" is consistently described in the OT and post-biblical Jewish literature as a daily offering. **"The one lamb thou shalt offer in the morning; and the other lamb thou shalt offer at even"** (Exod. 29:39). These were offered separately.

In summary, it is important to treat the phrases "evening and morning" and "morning and evening" differently, for they do not carry like or even similar connotations.

How Long is 2,300 Days?

The 2,300 days are not literal days, but prophetic. To confirm, just read the context of Daniel 8. The first symbols that were shown in Daniel 8 were the ram and goat. The angel said to Daniel the ram and goat respectively represent Medo-Persia and Greece. Then Daniel was shown the little horn arising in the latter time, meaning the end of Greece's reign. In other words, it's going to be the next kingdom after Greece. History confirms that Rome was the next kingdom after Greece, and the little horn's reign continued through the papal phase.

Then Daniel was shown the 2,300 days. These symbols were given to Daniel in chronological order. Therefore, the 2,300 days must take place after the rise and fall of the ram, goat, and little horn. Keep in mind that 2,300 literal days equals about six years. However, the Medes and Persians ruled the world from 539 to 331 BC. The nation of Greece ruled the world centuries after the life of the Prophet Daniel, from 331 to 168 BC. The Roman Empire ruled from 168 BC to AD 476. The papacy ruled from 538 to 1798. This confirms that the 2,300 days represent prophetic time based on the context.

Having established this, let's continue with our calculations. We must remember that in prophetic time, a day equals a year (see Num. 14:34 and

108 | *The Final Atonement*

Ezek. 4:6). According to this rule, 2,300 days equal 2,300 literal years. In Daniel's vision, the mighty angel of Jehovah solemnly affirmed to Daniel that at the end of the 2,300 evenings and mornings, the sanctuary would be cleansed.

When Do the 2,300 Days Start?

> **And I heard a man's voice between *the banks of* Ulai, which called, and said, Gabriel, make this *man* to understand the vision. So he came near where I stood: and when he came, I was afraid, and fell upon my face: but he said unto me, Understand, O son of man: for at the time of the end *shall be* the vision.... And the vision of the evening and the morning which was told *is* true: wherefore shut thou up the vision; for it *shall be* for many days. And I Daniel fainted, and was sick *certain* days; afterward I rose up, and did the king's business; and I was astonished at the vision, but none understood *it*.** (Dan. 8:16, 17, 26, 27)

We are told the vision of the 2,300 days was for many days and shut up. Specifically, the angel said it would extend to the time of the end. For what it's worth, similar verbiage is used later on in Daniel. **"But thou, O Daniel, shut up the words, and seal the book, *even* to the time of the end: many shall run to and fro, and knowledge shall be increased.... Many shall be purified, and made white, and tried; but the wicked shall do wickedly: and none of the wicked shall understand; but the wise shall understand"** (Dan. 12:4, 10).

We have verified, earlier in this book, and likely in our past studies of Bible prophecy, that we live in the time of the end. There is an element of mystery in Daniel 8, and though we have not yet determined the start of this time prophecy, we are at the point in earth's history when Daniel's previously cryptic messages can be more easily deciphered.

Daniel was seeking to know the details of the 2,300 days when he presented his prayer to God. In answer to his prayer, the angel Gabriel informs him of seventy weeks. Daniel seems confused about the seventy weeks, when compared with Jeremiah's prophesy of seventy years, as well as Gabriel's 2,300 days. It is all very difficult.

These seventy weeks have been "determined" (cut off). From what are the seventy weeks cut off? The angel Gabriel came to give him "skill and understanding." He informed him that he was to "consider the vision"—the vision of the previous chapter. Gabriel was telling Daniel the seventy weeks were cut off from the 2,300 days (evening and morning).

The Vision Of The Evening And Morning | 109

To understand when 2,300 days start, the answer is found the following verse: **"Know therefore and understand, *that* from the going forth of the commandment to restore and to build Jerusalem unto the Messiah the Prince *shall be* seven weeks, and threescore and two weeks: the street shall be built again, and the wall, even in troublous times"** (Dan. 9:25). The decree to rebuild Jerusalem came in the year 457 BC. This is when the king of Persia, Artaxerxes, permitted the Jews to return to Jerusalem. This is the date that starts the 2,300-day prophecy of Daniel 8.

How Does This Prophecy Concern Us?

Daniel 8 is divided into two parts. The first half contains symbols and prophecies and the second half contains the interpretations. Since Gabriel interpreted all the symbols, except for the 2,300 days, he returned later to explain this part of the prophecy to Daniel.

To reiterate, the 2,300 days are not literal, but prophetic, and equate to 2,300 years, around the end of the reign of the little horn power. Attention is now directed to the sanctuary. **"And he said unto me, Unto two thousand and three hundred days; then shall the sanctuary be cleansed"** (Dan. 8:14). The Jews knew what that terminology meant. The cleansing of the sanctuary alluded to the Day of Atonement, which was a period of judgment for them. Concerning this, the Scripture says:

> *The sacrifice we offer to God is our prayers and worship. Taking away the daily sacrifice, on a personal level, means taking away our right and freedom to worship God in purity and holiness.*

> **"And he shall make an atonement for the holy [place], because of the uncleanness of the children of Israel, and because of their transgressions in all their sins: and so shall he do for the tabernacle of the congregation, that remaineth among them in the midst of their uncleanness…And he shall go out unto the altar that [is] before the LORD, and make an atonement for it; and shall take of the blood of the bullock, and of the blood of the goat, and put [it] upon the horns of the altar round about. And he shall sprinkle of the blood upon it with his finger seven times,**

and cleanse it, and hallow it from the uncleanness of the children of Israel." (Lev. 16:16–19)

In putting together these clues, it is safe to conclude that the Day of Atonement has an antitypical equivalent that would unfold during the time of the end.

CHAPTER 10

The People of The Covenant

Moses has traced the evils that would result from a departure from the statutes of Jehovah. Calling heaven and earth to witness, he declared that if, after having dwelt long in the Land of Promise, the people should introduce corrupt forms of worship, bow down to graven images, and refuse to return to the worship of the true God, the anger of the Lord would be aroused, and they would be carried away captive and scattered among the heathen. This prophecy, fulfilled in part during the time of the judges, met a more complete and literal fulfillment in the captivity of Israel in Assyria and Judah in Babylon.

The apostasy of Israel developed gradually. From generation to generation, Satan made repeated attempts to cause the chosen nation to forget the commandments, statutes, and judgments that they promised to keep forever. The Lord spoke through Jeremiah:

> Return, thou backsliding Israel...*and* I will not cause mine anger to fall upon you: for I *am* merciful, saith the LORD, *and* I will not keep *anger* forever. Only acknowledge thine iniquity, that thou hast transgressed against the LORD thy God...Turn, O backsliding children, saith the LORD; for I am married unto you... Thou shalt call me, My father; and shalt not turn away from me.... Return, ye backsliding children, *and* I will heal your backslidings. (Jer. 3:12–14, 19, 22)

God makes it clear that only by the most thorough heart reformation could the impending doom be averted. However, a refusal to heed His invitation of mercy brought to the impenitent nation the His judgments. What was God's pronouncement on His rebellious people?

> Then said Isaiah to Hezekiah, Hear the word of the LORD of hosts: Behold, the days come, that all that *is* in thine house, and *that* which thy fathers have laid up in store until this day, shall be carried to Babylon: nothing shall be left, saith the LORD. And of thy sons that shall issue from thee, which thou shalt beget, shall they take away; and they shall be eunuchs in the palace of the king of Babylon. (Isa. 39:5–7)

The Approached Doom

The capture mentioned in the following passage occurred in 606 BC:

> In the third year of the reign of Jehoiakim king of Judah came Nebuchadnezzar king of Babylon unto Jerusalem, and besieged it. And the Lord gave Jehoiakim king of Judah into his hand, with part of the vessels of the house of God: which he carried into the land of Shinar to the house of his god; and he brought the vessels into the treasure house of his god. And the king spake unto Ashpenaz the master of his eunuchs, that he should bring *certain* of the children of Israel, and of the king's seed, and of the princes... (Dan. 1:1–3)

When the first captivity occurred, among those first taken were Daniel, Hananiah, Mishael, and Azariah. Although Isaiah prophesied the captivity, he did not say how long it would be. It was Jeremiah who prophesied how long it would last. **"For thus saith the LORD, That after seventy years be accomplished at Babylon I will visit you, and perform my good word toward you, in causing you to return to this place"** (Dan. 29:10).

The captivity lasted seventy years. Solomon's temple was depleted and desecrated by the Babylonians and finally destroyed in the days of

Zedekiah. **"To fulfil the word of the LORD by the mouth of Jeremiah, until the land had enjoyed her sabbaths:** *for* **as long as she lay desolate she kept sabbath, to fulfil threescore and ten years"** (2 Chron. 36: 21).

Jeremiah prophesied that Israel would be taken captive to Babylon for seventy years, and Jerusalem and its temple would be destroyed. He also predicted that at the end of this period, Babylon would fall. God would restore His people back to their eternal inheritance.

The Rise of Cyrus

Which king was to make the decree allowing the Hebrews to return home to rebuild their temple? **"Thus saith the LORD to his anointed, to Cyrus, whose right hand I have holden, to subdue nations before him; and I will loose the loins of kings, to open before him the two leaved gates; and the gates shall not be shut"** (Isa. 45:1).

More than a century before the birth of Cyrus, the pen of inspiration mentioned him by name, and a record was made of the actual work he would perform in taking the city of Babylon unaware and preparing the way for the release of the children Israel. **"Cyrus,** *He is* **my shepherd, and shall perform all my pleasure: even saying to Jerusalem, Thou shalt be built; and to the temple, Thy foundation shall be laid"** (Isa. 44:28). **"I have raised him up in righteousness, and I will direct all his ways: he shall build my city, and he shall let go my captives, not for price nor reward, saith the LORD of hosts"** (Isa. 45:13).

King Darius

Cyaxares, who was also called Darius, was the king of the Medes. His political union with Cambyses, the monarch of Persia, led to the downfall of Babylon. The expedition that brought about Babylon's fall was led by General Cyrus, the son of Cambyses. They completed the conquering of all three Babylonian provinces—Babylon, Lydia, and Egypt—in 538 BC. Darius the Median monarch ascended to the throne as the first emperor. The reign of Darius was honored of God. To him was sent the angel Gabriel **"to confirm and strengthen him"** (Dan. 11:1).

It was in the sixty-eighth year of Jewish captivity and the first year of Darius the king of the Medes that Daniel offered his prayer to God. However, in 536 BC, two years later, Darius died, but before his death, he made Cyrus the Persian general his successor. In that very same year, Cambyses I, Cyrus's father, also died. Cyrus was brought to the Persian throne. He then united the two kingdoms together.

114 | *The Final Atonement*

The first year of the reign of Cyrus marked the completion of the seventy years since the first company of Hebrews was taken by Nebuchadnezzar. Cyrus fulfilled what we read in Isaiah 44:28. Let us look at his decree:

> Now in the first year of Cyrus king of Persia, that the word of the LORD by the mouth of Jeremiah might be fulfilled, the LORD stirred up the spirit of Cyrus king of Persia, that he made a proclamation throughout all his kingdom, and *put it* also in writing, saying, Thus saith Cyrus king of Persia, The LORD God of heaven hath given me all the kingdoms of the earth; and he hath charged me to build him an house at Jerusalem, which *is* in Judah. Who *is there* among you of all his people? his God be with him, and let him go up to Jerusalem, which *is* in Judah, and build the house of the LORD God of Israel, (he *is* the God,) which *is* in Jerusalem. (Ezra 1:1–3)

Please note that Cyrus' decree only addressed the rebuilding of the temple. There was no explicit reference to the rebuilding of the city of Jerusalem, which included the wall and street. Then what does God imply through the prophecy that Cyrus would rebuild the temple and city of Jerusalem? What the prophecy seems to point out is that the project has two stages of implementation: first, the laying of the temple's foundation, which was to be accomplished by Cyrus, and second, the building of the city wall and street, which was to be accomplished by the Persian Empire. In what year was the second temple's foundation actually laid?

> From the first day of the seventh month began they to offer burnt offerings unto the LORD. But the foundation of the temple of the LORD was not *yet* laid.... Now in the second year of their coming unto the house of God at Jerusalem, in the second month, began Zerubbabel the son of Shealtiel, and Jeshua the son of Jozadak, and the remnant of their brethren the priests and the Levites, and all they that were come out of the captivity unto Jerusalem; and appointed the Levites, from twenty years old and upward, to set forward the work of the house of the LORD. (Ezra 3:6, 8)

The foundation of the temple was laid in the second year of Cyrus (534 BC). The project was entrusted to Zerubbabel, a descendant of King David, and Joshua the priest. The building continued even until the reign of Cyrus' eldest son, Cambyses II (the grandson of Cambyses I).

During the reign of Cambyses II. the work on the temple progressed slowly. During the reign of the Smerdis (called Artaxerxes), the Samaritans induced the unscrupulous impostor to issue a decree forbidding the Jews to rebuild their temple. The Bible says, **"Now when the copy of king Artaxerxes' letter *was* read before Rehum, and Shimshai the scribe, and their companions, they went up in haste to Jerusalem unto the Jews, and made them to cease by force and power. Then ceased the work of the house of God which *is* at Jerusalem. So it ceased unto the second year of the reign of Darius king of Persia"** (Ezra 4:23–24).

What decree brought about the resumption of the building of the temple?

> *God makes it clear that only by the most thorough heart reformation could the impending doom be averted. However, a refusal to heed His invitation of mercy brought to the impenitent nation the His judgments.*

Then Darius the king made a decree, and search was made in the house of the rolls, where the treasures were laid up in Babylon. And there was found at Achmetha, in the palace that *is* in the province of the Medes, a roll, and therein *was* a record thus written: In the first year of Cyrus the king *the same* Cyrus the king made a decree *concerning* the house of God at Jerusalem, Let the house be builded, the place where they offered sacrifices, and let the foundations thereof be strongly laid…Let the work of this house of God alone; let the governor of the Jews and the elders of the Jews build this house of God in his place. Moreover I make a decree what ye shall do to the elders of these Jews for the building of this house of God: that of the king's goods, *even* of the tribute beyond the river, forthwith expenses be given unto these men, that they be not hindered.… I have made a decree, that whosoever shall alter this word, let timber be pulled down from his house, and being set up, let him be hanged thereon; and let his house be made a dunghill for this.… I Darius have made a decree; let it be done with speed. (Ezra 6:1–3, 7, 8, 11, 12)

Artaxerxes the King

It was during the reign of Darius that the temple was successfully rebuilt. Having established this point, the next issue is the building of the city of Jerusalem. The restoration of Jerusalem meant the restoration of the people to their homeland. The city represents the heart-beat and security of the land around; while the temple represents the heart-beat and security of the city. By whose decree was the city of Jerusalem rebuilt?

> Now this *is* the copy of the letter that the king Artaxerxes gave unto Ezra the priest, the scribe, *even* a scribe of the words of the commandments of the LORD, and of his statutes to Israel. Artaxerxes, king of kings, unto Ezra the priest, a scribe of the law of the God of heaven, perfect *peace*, and at such a time. I make a decree, that all they of the people of Israel, and *of* his priests and Levites, in my realm, which are minded of their own freewill to go up to Jerusalem, go with thee.... And thou, Ezra, after the wisdom of thy God, that *is* in thine hand, set magistrates and judges, which may judge all the people that *are* beyond the river, all such as know the laws of thy God; and teach ye them that know *them* not. And whosoever will not do the law of thy God, and the law of the king, let judgment be executed speedily upon him, whether *it be* unto death, or to banishment, or to confiscation of goods, or to imprisonment. (Ezra 7:11–13, 25, 26)

Artaxerxes began his reign in 464 BC, and he issued this decree in his seventh year (see 7:8). "In (Nehemiah 2:1) we have another Artaxerxes. We may safely identify him with Artaxerxes Macrocheir or Longimanus, the son of Xerxces, who reigned BC 464–425" (Bible Hub, http://1ref.us/ms, accessed March 13, 2018). Therefore, Artaxerxes' seventh year as king was 457 BC.

Ezra began to go up on the first day of the first month and arrived at Jerusalem on the first day of the fifth month, in the seventh year of Artaxerxes the king. Having arrived at Jerusalem, he appointed magistrates and judges and restored the Jewish commonwealth under the protection of the king of Persia, as he was fully authorized to do by the decree. This last decree restored the full Jewish government, making provision for the enforcement of their laws.

History confirmed: "The Persian Empire was founded by Cyrus in 536 BC, after they succeeded the Babylonian Empire. The first king of the

Persian Empire was Cyrus, who issued the famous decree for the Jews to return to their homeland to rebuild their Temple.

"Under Darius the second Temple of Zerubbabel was completed; and under Xerxes, or Ahasuerus, the events recorded in the Book of Esther in the Bible happened; under Artaxerxes the Jewish state was reformed by Ezra, and the walls of Jerusalem were rebuilt by Nehemiah. The capital of the Persian Empire was Shushan. The Empire lasted about 200 years, and came to an end in 330 BC" (Bible History Online, "The Persian Empire", http://1ref.us/mt, accessed March 13, 2018).

How many decrees were issued to bring about a complete fulfillment of Isaiah's inspired prophecy? **"And the elders of the Jews builded, and they prospered through the prophesying of Haggai the prophet and Zechariah the son of Iddo. And they builded, and finished** *it,* **according to the commandment of the God of Israel, and according to the commandment of Cyrus, and Darius, and Artaxerxes king of Persia"** (Ezra 6:14).

It was God's commandment that counted, and it took the decree of three kings before God counted it as one commandment. The first decree was made by Cyrus in 536 BC. This pertained to the temple. The second decree was made in the year 520 BC. The decree of Darius Hystaspes provided for the continuation of the work hindered by Smerdis, and by this decree the building was completed. The third and final decree was issued by Xerxes (or Ahasuerus) in 457 BC, restoring the Jewish commonwealth and rebuilding the city of Jerusalem.

Seventy Weeks Prophecy

In the light of what we just examined, let's direct our attention to Daniel's seventy-week prophecy . Having determined that the decree of Cyrus marked the end of the seventy years of Jeremiah's prophecy, does it also mark the beginning of Daniel's seventy-week prophecy? If not, why not? What is the goal and purpose of the seventy weeks?

> **Seventy weeks are determined upon thy people and upon thy holy city, to finish the transgression, and to make an end of sins, and to make reconciliation for iniquity, and to bring in everlasting righteousness, and to seal up the vision and prophecy, and to anoint the most Holy. <u>Know therefore and understand,</u>** *<u>that</u>* **<u>from the going forth of the commandment to restore and to build Jerusalem unto the Messiah the Prince</u>** *shall be* **<u>seven weeks, and threescore and two weeks: the street shall be built again, and the wall, even in troublous times.</u> And after threescore and two weeks**

shall Messiah be cut off, but not for himself: and the people of the prince that shall come shall destroy the city and the sanctuary; and the end thereof *shall be* with a flood, and unto the end of the war desolations are determined. And he shall confirm the covenant with many for one week: and in the midst of the week he shall cause the sacrifice and the oblation to cease, and for the overspreading of abominations he shall make *it* desolate, even until the consummation, and that determined shall be poured upon the desolate. (Dan. 9:24–27)

Verse 24 makes it clear that the goal of the seventy-week prophecy is six-fold in nature. Here is a list of the six things that are to be accomplished:

1. **To finish the transgression**
2. **To make an end of sins**
3. **To bring in everlasting righteousness**
4. **To make reconciliation (atonement) for iniquity**
5. **To seal up the vision and prophecy**
6. **To anoint the most holy**

This time period pertains to the Jewish people. There is an ambiguous mistranslation at the beginning of the passage. The word "determined" is from the Hebrew word *chathak*, which literally means "to cut off" or "to divide." The reason the translators did not translate it that way is because they failed to go back to the vision of Daniel 8. They could not determine from what it was cut off. Seventy weeks must be cut off from some longer period of time. Was there a longer period of time before the seventy weeks?

Yes. The longer period of time is no other than the 2,300 days, first mentioned to Daniel by Gabriel in the vision for the cleansing of the temple as he was meditating on the plight of his fellow Jews. He knew the number of years Israel would remain in captivity and saw that the end of the captivity was in sight. Therefore, he began to pray:

And whiles I *was* speaking, and praying, and confessing my sin and the sin of my people Israel, and presenting my supplication before the LORD my God for the holy mountain of my God; Yea, whiles I *was* speaking in prayer, even the man Gabriel, whom I had seen in the vision at the beginning, being caused to fly swiftly, touched me about the time of the evening oblation. And he informed *me*, and talked with me, and said, O Daniel, I am now come forth

The People Of The Covenant | 119

> to give thee skill and understanding. At the beginning of thy supplications the commandment came forth, and I am come to show *thee*; for thou *art* greatly beloved: therefore understand the matter, and consider the vision. (Dan. 9:20–23)

To which vision is Gabriel referring? The vision in Chapter 8 that relates to the evening and morning. Here we are told that he returns to finish the explanation of Daniel's previous vision and supply the meaning of 2,300 days,

Verse 25 provides the time parameter for the fulfillment of the prophecy. We learned from this verse the point of reckoning—the going forth of the commandment or decree to restore and build Jerusalem. Please note that the angel stated categorically that it was this decree, not the decree to rebuild the temple. It's worthwhile to note the three different decrees:

1. **First decree by Cyrus in 536 BC pertains to the building of the temple**
2. **Second decree Darius in 520 BC continued the work, hindered by Smerdis, and completed the building**
3. **Third decree by Xerxes in 457 BC restored the Jewish common wealth and rebuilt the city**

It is the third and last decree that culminates all that was commanded by God and fulfills verse 25. The decrees embrace three grand objectives: the building of the temple, the restoring of the Jewish commonwealth, and the building of the street and wall.

The first phrase in verse 26 says that the Messiah would be "cut off" after the sixty-two prophetic weeks. Added to the first seven weeks, this makes sixty-nine prophetic weeks. This verse introduces an evil prince who will destroy the city (Jerusalem) and sanctuary (where sacrifices are offered). Who is this coming prince? Many believe it is the final antichrist who will appear at the end of the age. However, we are told in this verse that the city and sanctuary are to be destroyed by the people of the prince who is to come.

Verse 27 then says that he shall confirm a covenant with many for one week. An important question is, "To whom does the pronoun 'he' refer?" Many believe that "he" refers to the prince mentioned in verse 26. This prince, it is believed, will establish some kind of covenant which will be broken "in the middle of the week" (after three and a half years).

However, a careful reading shows that "he" does not refer to the prince, but rather the Messiah. Notice the phrase "the people of the prince." It is not grammatically correct to assign the singular pronoun "he" in verse 27 to the plural "people" in verse 26, so who are these people of the prince who is to come and destroy the city and sanctuary? History attests that it was the Roman Empire that destroyed Jerusalem and the Jewish temple in AD 70.

Thus, one cannot assume the prince to be the antichrist. The Roman armies cannot be said to belong to an evil prince who was to appear in the last seven years of earth's history. It is unfitting to thus speak of the Roman armies who attacked Jerusalem in AD 70. These armies cannot be said to belong to a prince who has not even appeared, although nearly 2,000 years have passed.

The genitival relationship (people of the prince) clearly shows that the people and prince are contemporaries. The people belong to the prince; they are his people. Now, how can the Romans of AD 70 be said to belong to a prince who has not yet appeared? They are not his people; they belong to a prince who is their contemporary. Suppose that this prince should appear upon the scene of history. He cannot look back to the armies of Titus and call them his armies.

Using a modern example, Mussolini could not have spoken of the armies of Titus as being his own armies. This language itself rules out this interpretation. Simply put, the "prince" who is to come (i.e., who is future to Daniel), is Titus, the Roman general, whose armies destroyed the city of Jerusalem and its temple.

Are verses 26 and 27 of Daniel 9 sequentially related, or are they parallel descriptions of the same series of events? Close examination of these two verses reveals that they are structured in the poetic style of synonymous (or perhaps synthetic) parallelism in which verse 27 repeats and elaborates the content of verse 26. Thus, events that occur "after" the sixty-ninth week in verse 26 occur "in" the seventieth week of verse 27. There is no gap between the seven weeks and sixty-two weeks of verse 25, making it unlikely for there to be a gap between those sixty-nine weeks and the seventieth week.

There is another pronoun in verse 27 that also requires an explanation. In the New King James Version, we see the phrase "one who makes desolate." Who or what is this "one"?

The Overspreading Of Abomination

"And...for the overspreading of abominations he shall make *it* desolate, even until the consummation, and that determined shall be poured upon the desolate" (Dan. 9:27). The term "overspreading" can also be translated "wing" or "shirt" (Hebrew *kanaph*). What in the world can the words "overspread," "wing," and "shirt" have in common?

In Scripture, "wings" are referred to as a form of protection. The same goes for articles of clothing. In the beautiful words of the psalmist, we find the following: **"He shall cover thee with his feathers, and under his wings shalt thou trust"** (Ps. 91:4).

The word "abomination" was commonly used by the Israelites. The Hebrew root is *shaqats*, which means "to be filthy," "to loathe," or "to abhor." It is most often used to describe idolatrous worship practices, especially those most offensive to a sense of decency and morality. With this understanding, our next question is, "Who is the primary focus of Daniel's prophetic words?

For more than 1,000 years, the Jewish nation abused God's mercy and invited His judgments. They rejected His warnings and slayed His prophets. In every age, there is given to them their day of light and privilege, a probationary time in which they may become reconciled to God. However, they often despised God's ways of reconciliation.

For these same sins, the people of Christ's day made themselves responsible by following the same course. In the rejection of their present mercies and warnings lay the guilt of that generation. The fetters which the nation had been forging for centuries, the people of Christ's day were fastening upon themselves. There is a limit to this grace. Jesus said:

> **O Jerusalem, Jerusalem, which killest the prophets, and stonest them that are sent unto thee; how often would I have gathered thy children together, as a hen** *doth gather* **her brood under** *her* **wings, and ye would not! Behold, your house is left unto you desolate: and verily I say unto you, Ye shall not see me, until** *the time* **come when ye shall say, Blessed** *is* **he that cometh in the name of the Lord.** (Luke 13:34, 35)

For centuries, the judgment of God for the abomination of His covenant people has been overspread with the pleading of mercy. Mercy may plead for years and be slighted and rejected, but there comes a time when she makes her last plea. The angel said to Daniel, **"He shall make** *it* **desolate, even until the consummation, and that determined shall be poured upon the desolate"** (Dan. 9:27). To whom does the pronoun "he" in this verse refer? Students of prophecy believe that "he" refers to the prince mentioned in verse 25, and this prince is Christ the Messiah. The consummation points to the end of that which was to come upon the Jewish nation. Sad was the fate of those who rejected their hope of salvation.

Grammatically, it makes sense that all reference to "he" in the above verse point to the same person throughout the text—Jesus Christ. The "it" that is made "desolate" refers to the Jewish sanctuary. How did Christ make the Jewish sanctuary desolate?

The Jewish leaders committed "abominations" by instigating the death of God's dear Son, and their evil deed brought upon them terrible consequences. When Jesus cried out "It is finished" (John 19:30), the entire Jewish temple service, including its sacrifices, ceased to be of value in the sight of God. Christ's death made it desolate. Finally, in AD 70, the Roman armies, led by Titus, came and finished the job by completing the desolation.

Jesus clearly predicted the events of AD 70 when He forewarned His disciples, saying, **"And when ye shall see Jerusalem compassed with armies, then know that the desolation thereof is nigh"** (Luke 21:20).

In conclusion, may God help us learn these lessons from the temple. Jesus Christ's death means everlasting salvation to those who yield to His love, repent of their sins, and have faith in His sacrifice, but for those who choose abominations, remain in sin, and reject His grace, eternal desolation is the inevitable, terrible consequence.

CHAPTER 11

Prophetic Time

This chapter takes us through multiple time periods. The first is the fourteen generations, or 560 years, to Christ. The other two are the 2,300 years and 70 weeks/490 years of Daniel's prophecies. Fasten your seat belts! We're going to explore some fascinating biblical history. First, we'll begin with the book of Matthew. **"So all the generations from Abraham to David *are* fourteen generations; and from David until the carrying away into Babylon *are* fourteen generations; and from the carrying away into Babylon unto Christ *are* fourteen generations"** (Matt. 1:17).

The Fourteen Generations to Christ

What is the significance of the final fourteen generations in Matthew's account of Jesus' genealogy? Does it fulfill a specific prophecy? Does the number fourteen itself hold any special meaning? How would a first-century Jewish reader interpret this?

How does the Bible define a generation? Although the Bible does not give a direct answer in regards to the length of a generation, we can derive some observations. Scripture shows that the length of a generation varies, depending on the historical period. The early history of humanity shows longer generations because people lived much longer.

> *For more than 1,000 years, the Jewish nation abused God's mercy and invited His judgments.*

The NT opens with the genealogy from Abraham to Christ. These three groupings are all considered fourteen generations. When looking at the average generation for each group, we find that the generation length differs. God said to Abraham that after 400 years, He would deliver Israel, and Israel was delivered in the fourth generation, thus making one generation 100 years (see Gen. 15:13–16).

Later, the length of generation was reduced to 40 years. **"And the LORD'S anger was kindled against Israel, and he made them wander in the wilderness forty years, until all the generation, that had done evil in the sight of the LORD, was consumed"** (Num. 32:13).

"Forty years long was I grieved with *this* generation, and said, It *is* a people that do err in their heart, and they have not known my ways" (Ps. 95:10). **"When your fathers tempted me, proved me, and saw my works forty years. Wherefore I was grieved with that generation, and said, They do alway err in *their* heart; and they have not known my ways"** (Heb. 3:9, 10).

Therefore, the fourteen generations from Babylon to Christ are 560 literal years. With that said, what particular date is the starting point? Here is a clue we are given in the Holy Scripture: **"Consider now from this day and upward, from the four and twentieth day of the ninth *month*, even from the day that the foundation of the LORD'S temple was laid, consider *it*"** (Hag. 2:18).

Why was the prophet strictly commanded to consider this time? This is the clue we are given in God's Word: **"And again the word of the LORD came unto Haggai in the four and twentieth *day* of the month, saying, Speak to Zerubbabel, governor of Judah, saying, I will shake the heavens and the earth"** (vs. 20, 21).

After shaking the heaven and the earth, what happens next? **"And I will shake all nations, and the desire of all nations shall come: and I** will fill this house with glory, saith the LORD of hosts…The glory of this latter house shall be greater than of the former, saith the LORD of hosts: and in this place will I give peace, saith the LORD of hosts" (vs. 7–9).

This prophecy is connected to Christ's first advent. We are told that from the moment Zerubbabel laid the foundation of the second temple, the countdown to the coming of the Desire of All Nations (Jesus) started, and His personal presence in the second temple would hallow the precincts of the temple, rendering the glory of this latter house greater than that of the former. When did the Jews actually lay the foundation of the second temple that Jesus Christ graced with His presence?

> From the first day of the seventh month began they to offer burnt offerings unto the LORD. But the foundation of the temple of the LORD was not *yet* laid.… Now in the second year of their coming unto the house of God at Jerusalem, in the second month, began Zerubbabel the son of Shealtiel, and Jeshua the son of Jozadak, and the remnant of their brethren the priests and the Levites, and all they that were come out of the captivity unto Jerusalem; and appointed the Levites, from twenty years old and upward, to set forward the work of the house of the LORD. (Ezra 3:6, 8)

The decree to rebuild the temple was issued at the beginning of the reign of Cyrus the Persian emperor in 536 BC, but the foundation of the temple was laid in the second year of his reign, which was 534 BC. Take 534 BC as your starting date, then add fourteen generations, or 560 years.

Your arrival date is AD 26. From BC to AD, one year must be added (there was no zero). Therefore, the date would be AD 27. After what event did Jesus enter the temple once He began His public ministry? "Now when all the people were baptized, it came to pass, that Jesus also being baptized, and praying, the heaven was opened" (Luke 3:21). "And Jesus being full of the Holy Ghost returned from Jordan, and was led by the Spirit into the wilderness…And Jesus returned [from the wilderness] in the power of the Spirit into Galilee: and there went out a fame of him through the entire region round about. And he taught in their synagogues, being glorified of all" (4:1, 14).

At His baptism, Jesus was anointed and officially became the Messiah or Christ. He entered the temple and began His public ministry. The living presence of the One in whom dwelt the fullness of the Godhead bodily, who was God himself manifest in the flesh, made the glory of the latter house greater than that of the former.

The 2,300 Days and Seventy Weeks

Is there any connection between the 2,300 days of Daniel 8 and seventy weeks of Daniel 9? Let us first confirm an important point. In our previous analysis of these two important prophetic times, we noted how each is closely linked to the Jewish nation, Jerusalem, and their sanctuary. To get a complete picture of these prophetic times and their true understanding, we must note that the prophecy of Daniel 9 covers some of the same history that Daniel 8 does. Since Gabriel interpreted all the symbols in Daniel 8 to the prophet, except the 2,300 days, he returned to explain the 2,300 days in Daniel 9.

Therefore, when the angel told Daniel to cut off seventy weeks, he was actually telling him to subtract that from the 2,300 days. However, there's no way you can subtract weeks from days without first changing the weeks into days.

There are seven days in a week. If we multiply seven by seventy, we get 490 days. If we subtract 490 days from 2,300 days, we have 1,810 days left. Now you can see that the 2,300 days were divided into two sections: the first 490 days were allotted to the Jews. It can be said that the remaining 1,810 days (years) were allotted to the Gentiles.

It is interesting to note that any time the Jews were taken captive by Gentiles, the duration of their captivity was always timed. For instance, their bondage in Egypt lasted 400 years; Babylon, seventy years. From our study so far, in connection with the restoration of the Jews after the Babylonian captivity, you can see two segment of times were given, and we all can attest to the fact that the Jews again went into another captivity, which was predicted by Jesus: **"And they shall fall by the edge of the sword, and shall be led away captive into all nations: and Jerusalem shall be trodden down of the Gentiles, until the times of the Gentiles be fulfilled"** (Luke 21:24).

Thus, their captivity was timed and referred to as the times of the Gentiles. Having established this, let's go to our calculations. We must remember that in prophetic time, a day stands for a year. **"I have appointed thee each day for a year"** (Ezek. 4:6). According to this protocol, 2,300 days are equal to 2,300 literal years, so this section of 490 years is for the Jews, while 1,810 years are for the Gentiles, and the end of this time period brings us to the actual year when the second door in Revelation 11 shall be opened in heaven as the Lord cleanses the sanctuary, as revealed to Daniel by the angel Gabriel.

The seventy weeks are divided into three parts: seven weeks, sixty-two weeks, and one week. The connection shows that the seven weeks (forty-nine days/years) were allotted for the building of the street and wall, while sixty-two weeks (434 days/years) were to commence from where the seven weeks ended and extend to Messiah the Prince.

My dear reader, this date may not mean much to us unless we know what year the time prophecy was to begin. When do we begin the calculation of the 2,300 years? Here is the clue we are given in God's Word: **"Know therefore and understand,** *that* **from the going forth of the commandment to restore and to build Jerusalem…"** (Dan. 9:25).

> *Fasten your seat belts! We're going to explore some fascinating biblical history.*

The king that gave the commandment or decree for the Jews to rebuild Jerusalem and restore the entire ceremonial system was Artaxerxes. During what year of king Artaxerxes' reign was the decree given? **"And he came to Jerusalem in the fifth month, which** *was* **in the seventh year of the king"** (Ezra 7:8).

We discovered earlier that Artaxerxes' seventh year as king was 457 BC (he began his reign in 464 BC). This last decree restored the full Jewish government and made provision for the enforcement of their laws. This last decree, therefore, is the one from which we start the seventy weeks and 2,300 prophetic days.

Starting from 457 BC, the seven weeks (forty-nine days/years) allotted for the building of the street and wall concluded in 408 BC. From 408 BC, we add sixty-two weeks (434 days/years), and this brings us to AD 27. In this year, Jesus the Messiah was anointed by God at His baptism in the River Jordan. This year begins the final, prophetic week of Daniel 9:27. What was to be done in the last week of the seventy weeks? The Bible says, **"And he shall confirm the covenant with many for one week: and in the midst of the week he shall cause the sacrifice and the oblation to cease"** (Dan. 9:27).

Here we are told that Christ would confirm the new covenant with many within the space of seven days/years. However, in the middle of this seven-year period (the Hebrew for "midst" is *chetsiy*), He would cause the sacrifice to cease by means of His death. The middle of seven years is three and a half years, which takes us to the spring of AD 31. To clarify, the Passover lamb was annually slain in the spring. Jesus' baptism took place in the autumn of AD 27.

The week was divided into two halves by the death of Christ. Three and half years after the crucifixion would take us to the fall of AD 34, thus bringing the seventy weeks (490 years) to an end. The year AD 34 was the very year in which Stephen was stoned to death (see Acts 7). According to Catholic News Herald, we find the following: "On Dec. 26, the universal Church commemorates the death of St. Stephen in 34 A.D., the first man to give his life in witness to the faith. He is sometimes referred to as the 'protomartyr'" (Catholic News Herald, http://1ref.us/mw, accessed March 13, 2018).

Remember that 490 years were subtracted, or cut off, from the 2,300 years. This leaves a balance of 1,810 years. Adding this to AD 34, we arrive at the year 1844. What happened in that year? The second door was opened in heaven, and God's court was convened. Jesus Christ, our High Priest, began the last phase of His work of atonement—the cleansing of the sanctuary. **"And he said unto me, Unto two thousand and three hundred days; then shall the sanctuary be cleansed"** (Dan. 8:14).

This cleansing work is done by Christ who, with His own blood, blots out the forgiven sins of His redeemed—the sins which were recorded in the book of heaven. Through Christ's righteousness, as well as repentance, confession, and surrender, our lives can be prepared for eternity so that we are declared right with God at the judgment.

CHAPTER 12

October 22, 1844

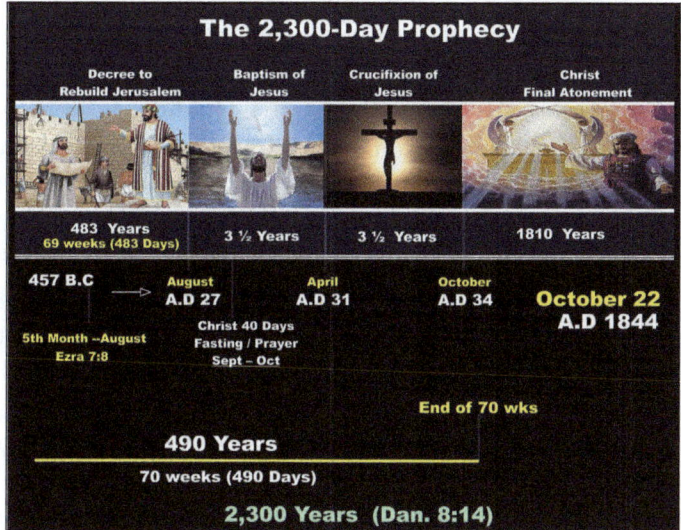

On what particular date in 1844 was this second door opened? On what date was the Day of Atonement? Does the Scripture in any way provide any clues? Can we determine this date through other key Bible events, like the season and month Jesus was born?

The Wise men from the East

"Now when Jesus was born in Bethlehem of Judaea in the days of Herod the king, behold, there came wise men from the east to Jerusalem" (Matt. 2:1). We read that the wise men from the east went to Jerusalem to inquire of the birth of Jesus. They finally were led by the star to find Jesus in Bethlehem. Did you notice the above Bible verse states that the wise men came into Jerusalem when Jesus was born? It did not say they came a year later, or a month later, but when He was born. With that said, when was Jesus born?

The phrase "when Jesus was born" is an aorist participle in Greek. It can be translated as "when Jesus was born" or "after Jesus was born." Aorist participles are frequent in the New Testament. With aorist participles, the action of the participle "Jesus was born" is closely followed by the action of the main verb in the phrase "wise men came to Jerusalem." Looking at it, there was not a significant time period between the times Jesus was born and the wise men came into Jerusalem.

The Killing of Children

Herod sent forth a horrifying decree. **"Then Herod, when he saw that he was mocked of the wise men, was exceeding wroth, and sent forth, and slew all the children that were in Bethlehem, and in all the coasts thereof, from two years old and under, according to the time which he had diligently enquired of the wise men"** (v. 16). He did not know when Jesus was born. Just because he ordered that children two years old and younger should be killed does not mean that Jesus was two years old at that time. Herod evidently thought that Jesus could have been a newborn baby. This explains the range in his decree.

Consider the fact that nine times in Matthew 2:8–21, Jesus is called a "young child." A baby is also called a young child. The term "young child" can mean an "infant" (Greek *paidion*). *Paidion* is used for John the Baptist when he was eight days old (see Luke 1:59, 66, 76, 80). It is used for Jesus when he was born (see 2:17), eight days old (see v. 21), and forty days old (see vs. 27, 40). In fact, *paidion* is used for Jesus when the shepherds were there on the night of His birth. Something else to keep in mind is that just because the wise men found Jesus in a house (see Matt. 2:11) and not in a stable or an inn does not mean they left the stable. From the pen of inspiration, we are told:

> The wise men departed alone from Jerusalem. The shadows of night were falling as they left the gates, but to their great joy they again saw the star, and were directed to Bethlehem. They had received no such intimation of the lowly estate of Jesus as was given to the shepherds.... At Bethlehem they found no royal guard stationed to protect the newborn King. None of the world's honored men were in attendance. Jesus was cradled in a manger. His parents, uneducated peasants, were His only guardians. (White, *The Desire of Ages*, p. 63)

The Day of Circumcision

Another proof of when Jesus was born is the account of His eighth-day circumcision and purification. Luke clearly stated, **"And when eight days were accomplished for the circumcising of the child, his name was called JESUS, which was so named of the angel before he was conceived in the womb"** (Luke 2:21). This account suggests that Jesus was named eight days after His birth. Matthew's account placed the sequence of the birth and naming of Jesus before the arrival of the wise men. Furthermore, it was shortly after the departure of the wise men that an angel spoke to Joseph in a dream to flee to Egypt.

Matthew could have used another word in the place of "young," but he chose the Greek word that means "infant." The age of an infant child ranges from newborn to one year old. Jesus was called a young child or infant before he was brought into Egypt by Joseph and Mary (see Matt. 2:8–15).

Moses and Pharaoh

Additional evidence that Jesus was only a few months old when the death decree for all male children two years and under was issued by Herod is in the account of Moses.

> **But when the time of the promise drew nigh, which God had sworn to Abraham, the people grew and multiplied in Egypt, Till another king arose, which knew not Joseph. The same dealt subtly with our kindred, and evil entreated our fathers, so that they cast out their young children, to the end they might not live. In which time Moses was born, and was exceeding fair, and nourished up in his father's house three months: And when he was cast out, Pharaoh's daughter took him up, and nourished him for her own son.** (Acts 7:17–21)

Consider that Moses was three months old during the crisis when the Hebrew parents cast out their young children. The word "young" comes from the Greek *brephos* (meaning "babe," "infant," or even "embryo"). Moses was a type of Christ.

Duration of Purification

How long are the Jewish days of purification? God said to Moses:

> **Speak unto the children of Israel, saying, If a woman have conceived seed, and born a man child: then she shall be unclean**

seven days; according to the days of the separation for her infirmity shall she be unclean. And in the eighth day the flesh of his foreskin shall be circumcised. And she shall then continue in the blood of her purifying three and thirty days; she shall touch no hallowed thing, nor come into the sanctuary, until the days of her purifying be fulfilled. But if she bear a maid child, then she shall be unclean two weeks, as in her separation: and she shall continue in the blood of her purifying threescore and six days. And when the days of her purifying are fulfilled, for a son, or for a daughter, she shall bring a lamb of the first year for a burnt offering, and a young pigeon, or a turtledove, for a sin offering, unto the door of the tabernacle of the congregation, unto the priest. (Lev. 12:2–6)

The purification period for a Jewish mother who gave birth to a male or female child was forty or eighty days, respectively.

Herod's Death

Jesus was still called a young child or infant after the death of Herod. "But when Herod was dead, behold, an angel of the Lord appeareth in a dream to Joseph in Egypt, Saying, Arise, and take the young child and his mother, and go into the land of Israel: for they are dead which sought the young child's life. And he arose, and took the young child and his mother, and came into the land of Israel" (Matt. 2:19–21). According to history, Herod died in the year 4 BC. "The life of Herod the Great—king of ancient Judea—was the stuff of legend, but the cause of his grisly death more than 2,000 years ago has been a mystery.… Herod (73 BC–4 BC)…" (National Geographic News, http://1ref.us/ne, accessed March 13, 2018).

After the death of Herod, to where did Jesus' parents return? "But when he heard that Archelaus did reign in Judaea in the room of his father Herod, he was afraid to go thither: notwithstanding, being warned of God in a dream, he turned aside into the parts of Galilee: And he came and dwelt in a city called Nazareth: that it might be fulfilled which was spoken by the prophets, He shall be called a Nazarene" (vs. 22, 23).

After the Days of Purification

After Joseph and Mary returned from Egypt to Nazareth, in what special ritual did they engage? "And when the days of her purification according to the law of Moses were accomplished, they brought him to Jerusalem, to present *him* to the Lord" (Luke 2:22). The Bible says Jesus was brought to Jerusalem after the days of purification for a dedication service. After this religious ceremony, to where did Joseph and Mary, Jesus' parents, return? **"And when they had performed all things according to the law of the Lord, they returned into Galilee, to their own city Nazareth"** (v. 39).

Season and Month of Christ's Birth

Can we determine the season and month in which Jesus was born? Yes, we can. With all the above Bible clues, we can unravel this web. The Jewish historian Flavius Josephus tells us that Herod died shortly after an eclipse of the moon before the Passover (see *The Antiquities of the Jews*, book XVII, chapter VI, end of fourth paragraph). In the year 4 BC, a partial eclipse of the moon occurred around what we would know as March 13, shortly before the Passover, which was April 11.

Therefore, with the wise men's visit, Joseph and Mary's trip to Egypt, Herod's death, Joseph and Mary's return from Egypt, and Jesus' presentation in the temple after Mary's purification all happening within forty days of His birth, it would seem that His birth was around March/April in 4 BC.

John the Baptist's Ministry

At what particular time did John's public ministry begin?

> Now in the fifteenth year of the reign of Tiberius Caesar, Pontius Pilate being governor of Judaea, and Herod being tetrarch of Galilee, and his brother Philip tetrarch of Ituraea and of the region of Trachonitis, and Lysanias the tetrarch of Abilene, Annas and Caiaphas being the high priests, the word of God came unto John the son of Zacharias in the wilderness. And he came into all the country about Jordan, preaching the baptism of repentance for the remission of sins. (Luke 3:1–3)

Keeping Luke's account on the shelf for a moment, the historian Gibbon explains that prior to the death of Augustus, Tiberius was made a co-regent by Augustus, his adopted father, in AD 12, so he jointly reigned with him two years before his death. In AD 13, the powers held by Tiberius were made equal to Augustus' own powers, and in the event of the latter's passing, the former would simply continue to rule without an interregnum or possible upheaval. Augustus died in AD 14, at the age of seventy-six (Adventist Online, http://1ref.us/nf, accessed March 13, 2018). The joint reign of Tiberius Caesar and Augustus began in AD 12, so adding fifteen years would bring us to AD 27.

Christ's Baptism

How old was Jesus when He was baptized?

> Now when all the people were baptized, it came to pass, that Jesus also being baptized, and praying, the heaven was opened, And the Holy Ghost descended in a bodily shape like a dove upon him, and a voice came from heaven, which said, Thou art my beloved Son; in thee I am well pleased. And Jesus himself began to be about thirty years of age, being (as was supposed) the son of Joseph...
> (Luke 3:21–23)

Jesus was thirty years old when He got baptized. From the spring of 4 BC to the spring of AD 27 is thirty years. In what particular month was Jesus baptized? The key to understand this lies in the prophetic time of Daniel's prophecy. Gabriel states that this period was to begin with **"the going forth of the commandment to restore and to build Jerusalem"** (Dan. 9:25). The decree that gave the Jews full autonomy was issued by Artaxerxes in 457 BC. When did this decree go into effect? **"And he came to Jerusalem in the fifth month, which *was* in the seventh year of the king"** (Ezra 7:8).

The first month of the Jewish calendar, according to Exodus 12:1–2, begins in the spring. This corresponds with March/April on our modern Gregorian calendar. According to Ezra, the decree did not go into effect until five months into the year, and this corresponds to approximately August. In line with Daniel's prophecy, when we start from 457 BC, the actual date of Artaxerxes' decree, and progress 483 years (sixty-nine prophetic weeks), this brings us to August of AD 27.

Christ's Public Ministry

Our next question is, "Did Christ begin His public ministry immediately after His baptism?" The following Bible passage gives us a clue: **"And immediately the Spirit driveth him into the wilderness. And he was there in the wilderness forty days, tempted of Satan; and was with the wild beasts; and the angels ministered unto him"** (Mark 1:12, 13). He went into the wilderness to be alone and contemplate His mission and work, and for forty days and forty nights He fasted and prayed. By fasting and prayer, He braced Himself for the bloodstained path He must travel. In the face of temptation, He stood firm and overcame.

From this account, we can see He did not begin His ministry immediately, so when did He begin? **"And Jesus returned in the power of** the Spirit into Galilee: and there went out a fame of him through the entire region round about. And he taught in their synagogues, being glorified of all"** (Luke 4:14, 15). Forty days from August of AD 27, when He was baptized, extends the start of His ministry to September or October.

The Jews' Passover

Jesus attended the Passover feast after His baptism. **"And the Jews' passover was at hand, and Jesus went up to Jerusalem"** (John 2:13). At this Passover feast, there was a conversation between Jesus and the Jews. It was told to Jesus that the temple building had been in renovation for forty-six years. **"Then answered the Jews and said unto him, What sign shewest thou unto us, seeing that thou doest these things? Jesus answered and said unto them, Destroy this temple, and in three days I will raise it up. Then said the Jews, Forty and six years was this temple in building, and wilt thou rear it up in three days? But he spake of the temple of his body"** (vs. 18–21).

According to Josephus, the rebuilding of the inner part of the temple took a year and a half, and the outer enclosures took eight years. What year was the start of the renovation? We are told in the following historic account: "In 19 B.C. the master-builder, King Herod the Great, began the most ambitious building project of his life—the rebuilding of the Temple and the Temple Mount in lavish style" (Biblical Archaeology Society, http://1ref.us/mv, accessed March 13, 2018).

Keep in mind that the Jews were not referring to the number of years of reconstruction, but the number of years since the temple was rebuilt by Herod (for what it's worth, another retouching was conducted in AD 31). Using 19 BC as the starting point, when you go forward forty-six years into the future, you arrive at AD 28, which was the time of the Passover feast in John 2:13.

The Duration of Christ Ministry

How long was Jesus' ministry to last? **"And he shall confirm the covenant with many for one week: and in the midst of the week he shall cause the sacrifice and the oblation to cease"** (Dan. 9:27). The public ministry of Jesus, which began in October of AD 27, began the final prophetic week of Daniel 9:27. This means that Jesus would confirm the covenant for seven literal years. Jesus' ministry was to last three and a half years, based on the account of Daniel 9:27. He was crucified in the middle of the week. Three years from October of AD 27 brings us to October of AD 30, and an additional six month takes us to April of AD 31. The month of Abib was known as "The first month of the Jewish ecclesiastical year, corresponding nearly to the Gregorian April. After the Babylonish captivity this month was called Nisan" (Wikipedia, http://1ref.us/ng, accessed March 13, 2018).

The remaining three and half years brings us to October of AD 34. Remember that the 490-year prophecy was subtracted from the larger 2,300-year prophecy. This left a balance of 1,810 years. If added to October of AD 34, it takes us to October of 1844.

How Do We Arrive at October 22?

Under the Mosaic system, the cleansing of the sanctuary, or the Day of Atonement, occurred on the tenth day of the seventh Jewish month (see Lev. 16:29–34), when the high priest, having made an atonement for all Israel and removing their sins from the sanctuary, came forth and blessed the people. On which date, as we reckon, was the tenth day of the seventh month in 1844?

The rabbinical reckoning, which starts its new year on Nisan 1, the new moon closest to the vernal equinox, would be equivalent to March 21. However, the Karaite Jews, who are following Mosaic reckoning, placed the start of the new year on the first new moon after the vernal equinox, which would be equivalent to April 19. Who are the Karaite Jews? They are a back-to-the-Bible movement in Judaism. They arose in opposition to Rabbinic Judaism towards the end of the eighth century (AD).

The Rabbanites followed the traditions of the Talmud in addition to the Scriptures, but the Karaites abandoned all such traditions and went just by Scripture. This necessitated differentiating the dates on which they kept their festivals. The Karaite Jews' reckoning is more in line with the original, ancient, lunar Jewish calendar. Therefore, when we add six lunar months, or 177 days, to April 19, we arrive at October 13 as the first day of the seventh month, and an additional nine days would extend to the tenth day of the seventh month—October 22.

"The seventh Jewish month commenced with the appearance of the moon on the 13th of October, so that the tenth day of the seventh month synchronized with the 22nd of that month" (The Advent Shield, Boston, 1844–5, Vol. 1, 278).

Please note this important point: although there were new moons observed in all of the months leading up to the seventh month, there was no new moon to be observed on the night of October 12/13. Why? Technically, it has to do with how soon the new moon can be seen after conjunction—the point in time when the moon, earth, and sun are all in alignment and the moon cannot be seen (the conjunction is also called the "black moon").

Was there a black moon in October 1844? Yes, there was. The conjunction took place on the October 11 at 6:24 p.m., eastern time. The civil twilight was extended to 5:31 p.m., though the moon light set at 5:12 p.m. on October 12, but the first visible crescent was not seen on October 13, thus making it a dark day (this was observed in Portland, Maine—43.6615° N, 70.2553° W).

On the U.S. Naval Observatory website, the conjunction is referred to as the "new moon." However, in Bible times, the months did not start until the first crescent could be observed. "That the first day of a lunar month begins with the 'first appearance,' or phasis, of the moon - is a precise calendar principle" ("The 1844 Problem—As Checked By Astronomy," Box 2, Folder 4, Grace Amadon Collection).

Although there was no new moon to be observed that night, and the first visible crescent was not seen in Jerusalem or America, it was seen in other countries. This day still marks the first day of the seventh month. It is interesting to note that the solution of Daniel's prophecy is dependent upon the ancient, original Jewish form of luni-solar time, not the altered, modern, rabbinical Jewish calendar because the latter is based upon decisions that were unknown in the time of Christ.

He went into the wilderness to be alone and contemplate His mission and work, and for forty days and forty nights He fasted and prayed. By fasting and prayer, He braced Himself for the bloodstained path He must travel. In the face of temptation, He stood firm and overcame.

What happened in that year? The second door was opened in heaven, and God's court was convened. Jesus Christ, our High Priest, began the last phase of His work—the final atonement and cleansing of the sanctuary. October 22, 1844 is the end of the great prophetic time periods. It is a day when the types of the Mosaic sanctuary service met their antitypical fulfillment.

As we have already studied, the Day of Atonement is part of the cycle of Jewish ritual that involves three components.

CHAPTER 13

The Final Atonement

In our study so far, we saw that the sanctuary on earth teaches wonderful lessons about God's plan of redemption. That the earthly sanctuary was patterned after the heavenly sanctuary is an established fact in God's Word. That it was designed to be an object lesson for Israel and the world and teach us, through its symbols, how God solves the sin problem from the sanctuary above is incontrovertible.

Therefore, the sanctuary truth is the grand and radiant nucleus around which clusters other glorious constellations of divine truth. It opens to our understanding the plan of salvation. The lifting of the veil opened to our vision the hallowed glory of Christ's priestly ministry in the Most Holy Place of the heavenly sanctuary. This work corresponds with the earthly cleansing of the sanctuary and the annual Jewish atonement, which includes three components:

1. **THE BLOTTING OUT OF SINS**
2. **THE CLEANSING OF THE SANCTUARY**
3. **THE DAY OF JUDGMENT**

These are essentially one event, presented from three different points of view. In type, this great work was represented by the services of the Day of Atonement. It commenced when Christ, the Mediator, bursting the bands of the tomb, ascended on high to minister for us. He first entered the Holy Place where, by the virtue of His own sacrifice, He made an offering for the sins of humanity before God. With intercession and pleading, He presented before God the prayers, repentance, and faith of His people, purified by the incense of His own merits.

He next entered (on October 22, 1844) the Most Holy Place to make final atonement for the sins of the people, cleanse them, bring an end to wickedness, usher in everlasting righteousness, seal up the vision and prophecy, and anoint the most holy. His work as High Priest completes the divine plan of redemption.

The Work of Purification

The coming of Christ as our High Priest to the Most Holy Place for the cleansing of the sanctuary is the same event that is brought to view in the following prophecy: **"I saw in the night visions, and, behold, *one* like the Son of man came with the clouds of heaven, and came to the Ancient of days, and they brought him near before him"** (Dan. 7:13). This also parallels another prophecy: **"Behold, I will send my messenger, and he shall prepare the way before me: and the Lord, whom ye seek, shall suddenly come to his temple, even the messenger of the covenant, whom ye delight in: behold, he shall come, saith the LORD of hosts"** (Mal. 3:1).

The messenger of the new covenant is said to have come to His temple. What is He coming to do? **"But who may abide the day of his coming? and who shall stand when he appeareth? for he *is* like a refiner's fire, and like fullers' soap: And he shall sit *as* a refiner and purifier of silver: and he shall purify the sons of Levi, and purge them as gold and silver, that they may offer unto the LORD an offering in righteousness"** (vs. 2, 3). The purpose of the Lord's coming to His temple is to purify His children. The heavenly court is in session now. While the sins of penitent believers are being removed from the sanctuary, there is to be a special work of purification—putting away of sin—among God's people upon the earth in the last days of history.

The Bible says, "How much more shall the blood of Christ, who through the eternal Spirit offered himself without spot to God, purge your conscience from dead works to serve the living God" (Heb. 9:14)? "For this purpose the Son of God was manifested, that he might destroy the works of the devil. Whosoever is born of God doth not commit sin; for his seed remaineth in him: and he cannot sin, because he is born of God" (1 John 3:8–9). The children of God who are going to live upon the earth when Christ returns will all be holy. Their robes must be spotless and characters purified from sin by the blood of sprinkling.

When this special work of purification is accomplished, the followers of Christ will be ready for His appearing. "Then shall the offering of Judah and Jerusalem be pleasant unto the LORD, as in the days of old, and as in former years" (Mal. 3:4). Therefore, brethren, there should be an earnest searching of the heart. There should be united, persevering prayer, and through faith, a claiming of the promises of God. There should be, not a clothing of the body with sackcloth, as in ancient times, but a deep humiliation of the soul. We should humble ourselves under the mighty hand of God. He will appear to comfort and bless His true seekers.

Behold the Bridegroom

This event is also represented by the coming of the bridegroom to the marriage, as described by Christ in the parable of the ten virgins. "And at midnight there was a cry made, Behold, the bridegroom cometh; go ye out to meet him" (Matt. 25:6). The work of Jesus in the Most Holy Place is equated to the marriage—the union of humanity with divinity. The term "atonement" means "at-one-ment"—joined to Christ. The final atonement means that the union between Christ and His people is consummated and sealed.

In light of this, who can successfully contend that the final atonement is only a judicial act which brings no experience to the saints? The final atonement is, in reality, the fulfillment of Jesus' prayer recorded:

> That they all may be one; as thou, Father, art in me, and I in thee, that they also may be one in us: that the world may believe that thou hast sent me. And the glory which thou gavest me I have given them; that they may be one, even as we are one: I in them, and thou in me, that they may be made perfect in one; and that the world may know that thou hast sent me, and hast loved them, as thou hast loved me. (John 17:21–23)

The church has never yet experience that blessed state of unity and perfection for which Christ prayed. As the followers of Christ are today waiting for their Lord, we are once again called to enter by faith into the marriage of the Lamb. Those who are of humble and contrite spirit are being called to enter into the place of atonement to behold the glory of the Lord shining in the face of Christ. All of God's children are to understand Christ's work and follow Him by faith as He goes in before God. It is in this sense that they are said to go into the marriage.

Those who love and follow Christ with all their hearts and souls have nothing to fear about the judgment. Jesus will present the merits of His own shed blood to cover every confessed sin. We are living in earth's last hours.

"For the time *is come* that judgment must begin at the house of God: and if *it* first *begin* at us, what shall the end *be* of them that obey not the gospel of God" (1 Peter 4:17)? The judgment begins with those who profess to be God's people. Everyone is judged according to the records in the books of heaven. Each individual is accepted or rejected as determined by the answer to one question: Has the blood of Christ covered one's sins?

My beloved brethren, the time is short. How will our cases appear in the judgment? What is now our standing before God? Are we closely examining our own hearts? Are we, by repentance and confession, sending our sins beforehand to the heavenly sanctuary, that they may be blotted out when the times of refreshing shall come?

Peter says, **"Repent ye therefore, and be converted, that your sins may be blotted out, when the times of refreshing shall come from the presence of the Lord; And he shall send Jesus Christ, which before was preached unto you"** (Acts 3:19, 20). A careful look at this inspired statement shows that the work of blotting out sins precedes the outpouring of the latter rain. Before giving us the baptism of the Holy Spirit, our heavenly Father will try us to see if we can live without dishonoring Him.

The purification of our souls is a work which we cannot safely delay. We should take hold of it earnestly. Our salvation depends upon our sincerity and zeal. Let the cry be awakened in every heart— "What must I do to be saved?" "The third angel's message is swelling into a loud cry, and you must not feel at liberty to neglect the present duty, and still entertain the idea that at some future time you will be the recipients of great blessing, when without any effort on your part a wonderful revival will take place" (White, 1946, pp. 701–2).

Today you are to give yourselves to God, that He may make you vessels unto honor, and meet for His service. Today you are to give yourself to God, that you may be emptied of self, emptied of envy, jealousy, evil surmising, and strife, everything that shall be dishonoring to God. Today you are to have your vessel purified that it may be ready for the heavenly dew, ready for the showers of the latter rain; for the latter rain will come, and the blessing of God will fill every soul that is purified from every defilement. It is our work today to yield our souls to Christ, that we may be fitted for the time of refreshing from the presence of the Lord--fitted for the baptism of the Holy Spirit.... The Word of The Lord reveals the fact that the end of all things is at hand, and its testimony is most decided that it is necessary for every soul to have the truth planted in the heart so that it will control the life and sanctify the character. The Spirit of the Lord is working to take the truth of the inspired Word and stamp it upon the soul so that professed followers of Christ will have a holy, sacred joy that they will be able to impart to others. Our only safety is in being ready for the heavenly refreshing, having our lamps trimmed and burning.... Day by day we are to seek the enlightenment of the Spirit of God, that it may do its office work upon the soul and character. (White, *God's Amazing Grace*, p. 205)

Purifying, Vitalizing Power

"**Create in me a clean heart, O God; and renew a right spirit within me**" (Ps. 51:10).

The Lord is waiting to purify the heart. As we air out a room, we do not close the doors and windows and throw in some purifying substance; we open the doors and windows and let heaven's purifying atmosphere flow inside. Likewise, we are to open our hearts to Jesus to come in and do His work.

Let us plead with God that He may cleanse us with hyssop, wash us, and make us whiter than snow. He will restore unto us the joy of His salvation, put within us new hearts, a right spirit, and new song of praise into our mouths. Each soul must be daily, consistently in communion with Christ. This is the life of the soul; this gives us a daily experience that does indeed make our joy full. Those who have this union with Christ will declare it in spirit, word, and work. Any cleansed soul, born again, has a clear, distinct testimony to bear.

"If we say that we have no sin, we deceive ourselves, and the truth is not in us. If we confess our sins, he is faithful and just to forgive us *our* sins, and to cleanse us from all unrighteousness. If we say that we have not sinned, we make him a liar, and his word is not in us" (1 John 1:8–10). Please note that the moment we, through genuine prayer, confess our sins, we are pardoned and cleansed, and we stand before God's presence as though we have not sinned. It is therefore expected of us, from that moment, to maintain our clean record before God by continuing to live holy.

The Drowning Soul

One bright summer afternoon, a number of years ago, a story is told about a party of ladies and children that were eating at a fashionable restaurant on the wharf, enjoying both the food and scenery. As they were eating, their attention was suddenly attracted by a loud splash in the water, followed instantly by a piercing scream. As the startled crowd turned, they saw a young man struggling in the water. He could not swim, and in his frantic efforts to rescue himself and swim to shore, he was, with each struggle, sinking deeper and deeper into the water, while being pulled farther and farther out to sea.

Those who love and follow Christ with all their hearts and souls have nothing to fear about the judgment. Jesus will present the merits of His own shed blood to cover every confessed sin.

The ladies ran to and fro to find help, but they found only one person nearby who could render any assistance. He was an old sailor who had been standing motionless, watching the poor man drown before their very eyes. However, the entreaties of the ladies could not move him, not until he saw the young man cease trying to save himself. Finally, the young man's arms relaxed, his struggle began to cease, and his face plainly expressed that he had given up in despair. When he came up for air for the last time, a feeling of horror came over the little company of ladies as they were to become unwilling witnesses to his death.

However, it was not until all hope was gone that the brave sailor leaped into the water and, as that drowning man arose for the last time, seized and dragged him safely to shore. As the ladies gathered around him, he said, "I was compelled to wait until he ceased trying to save himself; for I could save him only when he was without strength."

Similarly, our Savior Jesus Christ can never save people until those people cease trying to save themselves and give themselves up solely to the power of Christ. "Everywhere there are hearts crying out for something which they have not. They long for a power that will give them mastery over sin, a power that will deliver them from the bondage of evil, a power that will give health and life and peace" (White, 1905, p. 143).

It is only when we fall helpless at the foot of the cross and no longer trust in our own strength and effort that we can obtain divine help from above. People cannot save themselves. A million years of good works will not secure eternity. Those who trust in their own power to be saved will die trying. Please don't be like those who, in foolishness, will die in their sins because they cannot let go, stop struggling to save themselves, and simply let Jesus save them.

My dear friend, do not allow anything to draw your attention from what must done to inherit eternal life. We must settle this issue for eternity. Always know that "In the struggle for eternal life, we cannot lean upon one another. The bread of life must be eaten by each one. Individually we must partake of it, that soul, body, and mind may be revived and strengthened by its transforming power" (White, 1923, p. 385).

Can you see how willingly Christ reaches out His great arm, lifts the drowning soul out of the water, and tenderly saves and purifies that person in the blood of the Lamb? He wants to reach out His arm to you, but He will not do it until you stop trying to save yourself. Surrender your will to Jesus today. Ask Him to save you. Surrender all your efforts and good works and let Jesus come into your life.

Jesus, the Lamb of God, took our sin and died on the cross. This reminds me of a story related by Pastor A.C. Dixon, the great Baptist preacher, who was born in the mountains of Virginia.

"Tom, I'll Love You Till I Die"

Years ago, in the aforementioned region, there was a certain school which no teacher could handle. The boys were so rough that teachers resigned. A young, gray-eyed teacher applied, and the old director scanned him, then said, "Young fellow, do you know what you are asking? An awful beatin'! Every teacher we have had for years had to take it."

He replied, "I'll risk it." Finally, he appeared for duty. One big fellow, Tom, whispered, "I won't need any help, I can lick him myself!"

The teacher said, "Good morning boys! We have come to conduct school, but I confess I do not know how unless you help me. Suppose we have a few rules. You tell me and I will write them on the blackboard."

One fellow yelled, "No stealing!"

Another yelled, "On time."

Finally, ten rules appeared. "Now," said the teacher, "a law is no good unless there is a penalty attached. What shall we do with the one who breaks them?"

"Beat him across the back ten times without his coat on."

"That is pretty severe, boys. Are you ready to stand it?" There was an uproar, then the teacher said, "School comes to order!"

In a day or so, "Big Tom" found that his dinner was stolen. Upon inquiry, the thief was identified—a little hungry fellow, about ten years old. The next morning, the teacher announced, "We have found the thief and he must be punished according to your rule—ten stripes across the back! Jim, come up here!"

The little fellow, trembling, came up slowly with a big coat fastened up to his neck and pleaded, "Teacher, you can lick me as hard as you like, but please don't make me take my coat off."

"Take that coat off; you helped make the rules."

"Oh, teacher, don't make me!" He began to unbutton, and what did the teacher behold? Lo, the lad had no shirt on, but strings for suspenders over his little, bony body. 'How can I whip this child,' he thought, 'but I must do something if I'll keep this school.' The classroom was as quiet as death. "How come you came to school without a shirt, Jim?

He replied, "My Father died and mother is very poor. I have only one shirt to my name, and she is washing that today, and I wore my brother's big coat to keep me warm."

The teacher, with the rod in his hand, hesitated. Just then, "Big Tom" jumped to his feet and said, "Teacher, if you don't object, I will take Jim's licking for him."

"Very well, there is a certain law that one can become a substitute for another. Are you all agreed?"

Off came Tom's coat, and after five hard strokes, the rod broke! The teacher bowed his head in his hands and thought, 'How can I finish this awful task?' Then he heard the entire school sobbing, and what did he see?

Little Jim had reached up and caught Tom with both arms around his neck. "Tom, I am sorry I stole your dinner, but I was awful hungry. Tom, I'll love you till I die for taking my licking for me! Yes, I'll love you forever!"

Treated as We Deserve

In like manner, Christ "the Sinless One, was treated as we deserve, that we, fallen and sinful, might be treated as He deserved" (White, 1913, p. 267). We have broken every rule and deserve eternal punishment, but Jesus Christ took our scourging for us, died in our stead, and now offers to clothe us with His garments of salvation. He suffered the agony of Gethsemane and the torture of His mock trial, where they beat Him until His back was like raw meat. They bowed down in mockery, hit Him in the head with a stick, and drove the crown of thorns into His brow, sending blood running down His face.

Watch Him stagger on His way to Calvary. The Son of God falls on His face in the dirt. He endures the horror of our sins while His blood runs, drop by drop, to the foot of the cross. Look at His quivering lips as He cries, "My God, My God, why hast Thou forsaking Me?" There He hangs, like a snake on a pole, writhing in agony, drinking the last drops of the wrath of God against sin. As Moses lifted up the serpent in the wilderness, Jesus was lifted up for you and me. Will you not fall at His feet and tell Him you will love and follow Him forever?

The Bible says, **"For God so loved the world, that he gave his only begotten Son, that whosoever believeth in him should not perish, but have everlasting life"** (John 3:16). "He gave Him [Christ] not only to bear our sins, and to die as our sacrifice; He gave Him to the fallen race. To assure us of His immutable counsel of peace…" (White, 1958, p. 45). God gave humanity the best gift of heaven so that the guiltiest transgressor should not be deterred from coming to Christ, however large the sin. Will you choose Him now as your personal Savior and follow Him all the way? You'll be so happy that you did.

The Closing Moment of Earth's History

Today the signs of the times declare that we are standing on the threshold of great and solemn events. Everything in our world is in agitation. Therefore, why not come to Christ now? This may sound too good to be real, but it is true. The Savior will make atonement for you and be your personal Advocate. Remember, Christ is the answer to all your sins and needs.

Dear reader, given this glorious inheritance that may be yours, what shall it profit you if you gain the whole world and lose your soul? What shall a man give in exchange for his soul? Absolutely nothing! Our best option is to accept Jesus as our personal Savior and consecrate ourselves to Him as His child. The most highly-valued treasure that you can give the Lord is your heart. Present to Him a complete offering by giving Him yourself. God's Word says:

> **Seeing then that we have a great high priest, that is passed into the heavens, Jesus the Son of God, let us hold fast *our* profession. For we have not an high priest which cannot be touched with the feeling of our infirmities; but was in all points tempted like as *we are, yet* without sin. Let us therefore come boldly unto the throne of grace, that we may obtain mercy, and find grace to help in time of need.** (Heb. 4:14–16)

God's appointments and grants in our behalf are without limit. The throne of grace is itself the highest attraction because occupied by One who permits us to call Him Father.... By His appointment He has placed at His altar an Advocate clothed with our nature. As our Intercessor, His office work is to introduce us to God as His sons and daughters. (White, *God's Amazing Grace*, p. 68)

Why not offer this pray: Lord Jesus Christ, I understand I have to invite You into my heart so that You can renew my mind and make me Your child. Therefore, I invite You to immediately come into my sinful heart and make me clean. I understand You have the power to keep me from falling. Please give me the grace to live a new life in Christ Jesus. Help me not to go back to my old, sinful life, but rather radiate your glory from this day on. This I pray in Christ's wonderful name. Amen!!!

Bibliography

"The 1844 Problem - As Checked By Astronomy", Box 2, Folder 4, Grace Amadon Collection

"Artaxerxes." Bible Hub. http://1ref.us/ms (accessed March 13, 2018).

The Bible Timeline. http://1ref.us/mt (accessed March 13, 2018).

Josephus, Flavius. *The Antiquities of the Jews*.

Macdonald, J.A. "The Decree of Cyrus." Bible Hub. http://1ref.us/mu (accessed March 13, 2018).

Ritmeyer, Leen. "The Temple Mount in the Herodian Period (37 BC–70 A.D.)" Biblical Archaeology Society. http://1ref.us/mv (accessed March 13, 2018).

"St. Stephen, the First Martyr, Remembered Dec. 26." Catholic News Herald. http://1ref.us/mw (accessed March 13, 2018).

Trivedi, Bijal P. "What Disease Killed King Herod?" National Geographic News. http://1ref.us/ne (accessed March 13, 2018).

White, Ellen G. *Counsels to Parents, Teachers, and Students*. Mountain View, CA: Pacific Press Publishing Association, 1913.

White, Ellen G. *The Desire of Ages*. Mountain View, CA: Pacific Press Publishing Association, 1898.

White, Ellen G. *Evangelism*. Washington, DC: Review and Herald Publishing Association, 1946.

White, Ellen G. *The Faith I Live By*. Washington, DC: Review and Herald Publishing Association, 1958.

White, Ellen G. *God's Amazing Grace*. Washington, DC: Review and Herald Publishing Association, 1973.

White, Ellen G. *Manuscript Releases*. Vol. 12. Silver Spring, MD: Ellen G. White Estate, 1990.

White, Ellen G. *The Ministry of Healing.* Mountain View, CA: Pacific Press Publishing Association, 1905.

White, Ellen G. *Patriarchs and Prophets.* Washington, DC: Review and Herald Publishing Association, 1890.

White, Ellen G. *Selected Messages.* Book 1. Washington, DC: Review and Herald Publishing Association, 1958.

White, Ellen G. *The Story of Jesus.* Nashville, TN: Southern Publishing Association, 1900.

White, Ellen G. *Testimonies to Ministers and Gospel Workers.* Mountain View, CA: Pacific Press Publishing Association, 1923.

TEACH Services, Inc.
P U B L I S H I N G

We invite you to view the complete
selection of titles we publish at:
www.TEACHServices.com

We encourage you to write us
with your thoughts about this,
or any other book we publish at:
info@TEACHServices.com

TEACH Services' titles may be purchased in
bulk quantities for educational, fund-raising,
business, or promotional use.
bulksales@TEACHServices.com

Finally, if you are interested in seeing
your own book in print, please contact us at:
publishing@TEACHServices.com

We are happy to review your manuscript at no charge.

www.ingramcontent.com/pod-product-compliance
Lightning Source LLC
Chambersburg PA
CBHW071212160426
43196CB00011B/2277